Are you religious? Do you sometimes feel you have been trapped into playing a game called "Church"? This book shows why religion has failed and points the way to being a Christian without being religious.

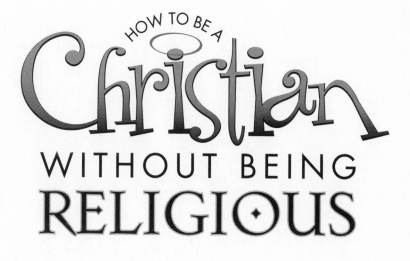

HOW TO BE A
Christian
WITHOUT BEING
RELIGIOUS

FRITZ RIDENOUR

Regal

From Gospel Light
Ventura, California, U.S.A.

PUBLISHED BY REGAL BOOKS
FROM GOSPEL LIGHT
VENTURA, CALIFORNIA, U.S.A.
Regal PRINTED IN THE U.S.A.

Regal Books is a ministry of Gospel Light, a Christian publisher dedicated to serving the local church. We believe God's vision for Gospel Light is to provide church leaders with biblical, user-friendly materials that will help them evangelize, disciple and minister to children, youth and families.

It is our prayer that this Regal book will help you discover biblical truth for your own life and help you meet the needs of others. May God richly bless you.

For a free catalog of resources from Regal Books/Gospel Light, please call your Christian supplier or contact us at 1-800-4-GOSPEL or www.regalbooks.com.

Cover and interior design by Robert Williams
Cover and interior illustrations by Curt Dawson

Library of Congress Cataloging-in-Publication Data
Ridenour, Fritz.
  How to be a Christian without being religious / by Fritz Ridenour.
    p. cm.
  ISBN 0-8307-2789-2 (trade paper)
  1. Bible. N.T. Romans—Criticism, interpretation, etc. 2. Young adults—Religious life. I. Title.
  BS2665.52 .R48 2002
  227'.106—dc21   2002001037

1 2 3 4 5 6 7 8 9 10 11 12 13 14 15 16 / 11 10 09 08 07 06 05 04

Rights for publishing this book in other languages are contracted by Gospel Light Worldwide, the international nonprofit ministry of Gospel Light. Gospel Light Worldwide also provides publishing and technical assistance to international publishers dedicated to producing Sunday School and Vacation Bible School curricula and books in the languages of the world. For additional information, visit www.gospellightworldwide.org; write to Gospel Light Worldwide, P.O. Box 3875, Ventura, CA 93006; or send an e-mail to info@gospellightworldwide.org.

CONTENTS

PREFACE

When this book first appeared, it was the late '60s—the decade of turbulence, rebellion and seeking freedom in drugs and the "new morality." Could the Bible offer understandable answers to the spiritual questions being asked by a generation that was tired of religious rules and churchianity?

As I studied the book of Romans, I realized that the apostle Paul had the answer. All that was needed was his letter to the church in Rome in a readable translation with just enough "commentary" to help the reader grasp the gist of his message: Being a Christian is not about obeying laws and rules. It's not about being "religious"—that is, trying to find God or please Him through your own futile efforts. Being a Christian is knowing—deep in your soul—that through His marvelous grace God has reached down and *found you*, and all you have to do is trust Him with your life.

With the invaluable editorial help of Georgiana Walker and the artistic genius of Joyce Thimsen, who did the original cartoons, *How to Be a Christian Without Being Religious* was created. God chose to bless it far beyond what anyone could have asked or thought, and there was a ready reception among millions of readers, young and old. Now it is over 30 years later. This "revised edition" contains updated illustrations and terminology; and the complete text of Romans has been changed from *The Living Bible* to the *New Living Translation*, a product of 90 scholars working for seven years to develop a translation that is accurate, easy to read and excellent for study.

The turbulent '60s are gone; the "anything goes" third millennium has arrived. We live in a secular society, a postmodern culture that claims there is no absolute truth of any kind, anywhere . . . that all ideas are equally valid . . . that knowing God is simply a matter of "becoming aware of your own divinity." But postmodernist New Age jargon can't fill the God-sized vacuum in each of us. Today's new interest in "spirituality" is really the same old self-effort to be religious and somehow feel okay about God (and, of course, yourself).

Today's spiritual questions are a bit different, but the answers are still the same. There *is* absolute truth—the gospel of Jesus Christ. You don't find God within your own sinful self. God, the creator and sustainer of the universe, finds you, and then His Holy Spirit comes into your life to give you hope, power and potential from beyond yourself.

If that sounds too simple, read on and see what Paul (and God) have to say. Paul was the most religious, law-abiding Pharisee on the planet; but one day, on that road to Damascus, he met Jesus Christ. Then Paul realized that being religious is hard work, a fruitless struggle, a tremendous burden. He became an apostle of the good news—being a Christian means the burden is off your back. You are free to become all that God has in mind for you to be.

Fritz Ridenour

Shouldn't a Christian Be Religious?

How to Be a Christian Without Being Religious almost sounds like a contradiction in terms. Christianity is called one of the world's great religions, is it not?

According to Webster's dictionary, a religion is a system of faith and of worship.

Christianity is certainly that.

According to Webster's dictionary, a religion is the service to and adoration of God expressed in forms of worship.

Christianity is certainly that, too.

According to Webster's dictionary, religion is devotion, fidelity, conscientiousness, an awareness or conviction of the existence of a supreme being, which arouses reverence, love, gratitude, the will to obey and serve.

Christianity is certainly that . . . and more.

It is the "more" that is behind the title of this book.

Christianity is more than a religion, because every religion has one basic characteristic. Its followers are trying to reach God, find God and please God through their own efforts. Religions reach up toward God. Christianity is God reaching down to man. Christianity claims that men have not found God but *that God has found them.* To some this is a crushing blow. They prefer religious effort—dealing with God on their own terms. This puts them in control. They feel good about "being religious."

Christianity, however, is not religious striving.

To practice Christianity is to *respond* to what God has done for you. The Christian life is a relationship with God, not a religious treadmill. Many Christians, however, behave like they really don't believe this. With form, formalism, ritual, legalism, rules, systems and formulas, we attempt to reduce Christianity to a religion—a system of some kind where works are really substituted for faith and trust, where law takes precedence over grace. We will not necessarily admit this, but it's true nonetheless. Instead of responding to God's love, we reach out for it on our own terms—and neatly keep God at arm's length while we do so.

But God will not stay at arm's length. When He comes into your life, He demands all of it. Away with religious pretense and pontificating. Away with your religious game called "Church" that you play so well every Sunday. God wants *all* of you—your heart, your soul, your body—as a living sacrifice to Him.

THIS BOOK
DEFINES "BEING
RELIGIOUS" AS
TRYING TO...

...REACH GOD

...FIND GOD

...PLEASE GOD

...THROUGH YOUR OWN FUTILE EFFORTS.

Is there a way to be a Christian without being religious? Is there some kind of surgical tool that will help us cut through the facade that leaves many of us feeling deep within that "Christianity is really 'being good' and if I'm not good, I haven't made the grade; and if I haven't made the grade, I'm left feeling frustrated, guilty and really not very happy with myself or my faith."

ALTHOUGH THEY MAY NOT REALIZE IT, MANY CHRISTIANS LIVE ON A RELIGIOUS TREADMILL...

...AND THE RESULT IS FRUSTRATION AND A FREQUENT SENSE OF FAILURE.

Yes, there is such a tool. It is a single book of the New Testament—Paul's letter to the Romans. In 16 brief chapters the great apostle shows you that Christianity is far more than a religion. He tells you who you really are, why you are living and how to get the most out of life. In short, in the following chapters you can find out for yourself how to be a Christian without being religious.

BUT THERE IS A WAY OFF THIS TREADMILL...

(UNLESS YOU REALLY LIKE THE TREADMILL TOO MUCH TO WANT TO CHANGE).

CHAPTER 1

Your Faith—Dead or Alive?

An old question . . . or is it? Let's define terms. Your faith is what you believe, the guiding principles and hope for your life. "Dead faith" is the kind that rests on little more than an intellectual system, dry and dusty credos, meaningless dogmas that have little to do with life as it really is. A "live faith" is just the opposite. To have a living faith means more than mental assent to a statement of beliefs. A living faith puts you in touch with God. A living faith has power. Paul opens his letter to Rome on this very same note.

ROMANS 1:1-17

[1]This letter is from Paul, Jesus Christ's slave, chosen by God to be an apostle and sent out to preach his Good News. [2]This Good News was promised long ago by God through his prophets in the holy Scriptures. [3]It is the Good News about his Son, Jesus, who came as a man, born into King David's royal family line. [4]And Jesus Christ our Lord was shown to be the Son of God when God powerfully raised him from the dead by means of the Holy Spirit. [5]Through Christ, God has given us the privilege and authority to tell Gentiles everywhere what God has done for them, so that they will believe and obey him, bringing glory to his name.

[6]You are among those who have been called to belong to Jesus Christ, [7]dear friends in Rome. God loves you dearly, and he has called you to be his very own people.

May grace and peace be yours from God our Father and the Lord Jesus Christ.

[8]Let me say first of all that your faith in God is becoming known throughout the world. How I thank God through Jesus Christ for each one of you. [9]God knows how often I pray for you. Day and night I bring you and your needs in prayer to God, whom I serve with all my heart by telling others the Good News about his Son.

[10]One of the things I always pray for is the opportunity, God willing, to come at last to see you. [11]For I long to visit you so I can share a spiritual blessing with you that will help you grow strong in the Lord. [12]I'm eager to encourage you in your faith, but I also want to be encouraged by yours. In this way, each of us will be a blessing to the other.

¹³I want you to know, dear brothers and sisters, that I planned many times to visit you, but I was prevented until now. I want to work among you and see good results, just as I have done among other Gentiles. ¹⁴For I have a great sense of obligation to people in our culture and to people in other cultures, to the educated and uneducated alike. ¹⁵So I am eager to come to you in Rome, too, to preach God's Good News.

¹⁶For I am not ashamed of this Good News about Christ. It is the power of God at work, saving everyone who believes—Jews first and also Gentiles. ¹⁷This Good News tells us how God makes us right in his sight. This is accomplished from start to finish by faith. As the Scriptures say, "It is through faith that a righteous person has life."

MUST A CHRISTIAN "ASSASSINATE HIS BRAIN"?

The opening paragraphs of Romans are strange words for a man who once hated Christianity. Paul was a Jew. He became a rabbi and was one of the religious conservatives of his time, the Pharisees. Immediately following Christ's death and resurrection in A.D. 33, Paul tried desperately to exterminate Christianity. Paul *knew* the Christians were wrong. They claimed that Jesus was the promised Messiah, the Savior—utter nonsense!

But on one of his campaigns to persecute Christians, Paul was struck to the ground by a blinding vision. He heard the voice of the living Christ, and he was changed. Paul did a complete about-face. He left the Pharisees (at the peril of his life) and became a devoted Christian, a "slave" of Christ (see Rom. 1:1).

And from the start Paul knew that being a Christian was not a matter of being "religious." He had plenty of religion as a Pharisee. He knew the Law like you know the alphabet. Still, the Law did not bring him peace. It did not put him in touch with the living God. But on that dusty road to Damascus, Paul got the message and found what he had been looking for all along (see Acts 9:1-19).

Paul became an acknowledged leader of the Early Church. He established groups of believers everywhere and wrote many letters to encourage them in their new faith. The epistle to the Romans is the only letter he wrote to a place he had not yet visited. Paul was anxious to reach Rome. He hoped to make the capital city of the Roman Empire a jumping-off place for more missionary work to the west—possibly Spain. While staying with friends in Corinth, Paul wrote to the church at Rome to give the members a better understanding of the meaning of the gospel. In these opening lines Paul wastes no time in getting around to why Christianity is a living faith.

> I am not ashamed of the gospel, because it is the power
> of God for the salvation of everyone who believes: first
> for the Jew, then for the Gentile (Rom. 1:16, *NIV*).

Paul was ready to share the gospel—the good news—because he knew that here was power. The gospel gives meaning to life. It can deliver the goods, giving us new purpose and focus. In Paul's day, people constantly sought salvation—peace of mind and heart, peace for their souls. People still seek salvation today, but somehow they miss the real message of the gospel. In far too many circles Christianity has been reduced to another religion, complete with rituals, rules and all necessary accouterments to "reach up to God." But this is not the gospel. There are several things the gospel is *not*.

THE GOSPEL IS NOT LAWS AND BURDENS.

The Gospel Is Not Laws and Burdens

It is not a list of religious *dos* and *don'ts*: you can't do this . . . you can't do that . . . hands off . . . mustn't touch . . . do this or die.

The Gospel Is Not Man-Made Ideas

Many people claim to worship God, but they keep Him very small—small enough to fit within the box they call their religion (or their brand of Christianity). But the gospel is not something man could have created; man just doesn't think that way.

The Gospel Is Not Anti-Intellectual

Some people reject Christianity, saying that they prefer a more sophisticated, intelligent belief system. The gospel, they claim, is for the ignorant or superstitious. Nonsense! You don't have to assassinate your brain to be a Christian, as many outstanding men and women can testify.

Dr. David Block, a well-known astronomer and professor, made this statement:

> Faith is never a leap into the dark. It is always based on evidence. When I studied relativity, relativistic astrophysics, cosmology . . . they pointed me to the fact that this whole universe is masterfully made, finely tuned and controlled

by the Great Designer. So it is on the basis of logic that we can understand that we live in a universe made by a personal God. It's logic from start to finish.[1]

Other respected scientists have openly professed the conviction that believing in God is not illogical. Dr. Hugh Ross, prominent astrophysicist and Christian apologist, has come to the forefront of modern science with the message that God's revelation of Himself in Scripture and in nature do not, will not, cannot contradict each other.[2] He says, "The more that astronomers learn about the origin and development of the universe, the more evidence they accumulate for the God of the Bible."[3]

Yes, Christianity is entered through the door of faith, but Jesus Himself also commanded us to love God with all our *minds* (see Mark. 12:30, *NIV*). Christianity is not a mindless religion.

So What Is the Gospel?

All right, we have looked at what the gospel is not. What then *is* the gospel? Let's look more closely at Romans 1:16-17 and see.

The Gospel Is Good News

Through Christ, God the creator involved Himself with mankind. He unleashed His mighty power and reached down to us, saying, "I love you, the burden is off your back! My Son died for your sin and guilt, and then He rose from the dead and conquered death forever. He *lives*, and through your faith in Him, you will live also."

The Gospel Is for Everyone

Paul says God's power works to save everyone who believes, Jew or Gentile (anyone who is not a Jew). The gospel is for *all*

THE GOSPEL
IS GOOD NEWS
FROM GOD.

undeserving sinners, from those who are just plain desperate to those who may feel they're "not so bad." The point is, we can't reach up to God on our religious own. The gospel is the only power that can make all of us totally right in God's sight.

The Gospel Saves Through Faith Alone

In the early sixteenth century, a devout Roman Catholic monk named Martin Luther struggled with his burden of sin. He tried with all his might to assure his salvation through the sacraments—attending Mass, making confessions, buying indulgences and doing penance. He did good works and fasted until he became a walking skeleton. He lived in an unheated cell in the bitter cold of winter and kept all-night prayer vigils.[4] He even began keeping long lists of his thoughts and actions to be sure he would confess all his misdeeds at confessionals. It didn't help. No matter how hard Luther tried, he felt no assurance of salvation, and his fear and guilt remained.[5]

This went on for years. Then, as a professor at Wittenberg University, Luther was studying the Scriptures and one verse leaped off the page to change his life (and the world) forever: "The just shall live by faith" (Rom. 1:17, *NKJV*). That started Luther on the road to assurance. As he spent longs hours pondering Romans 1:17, he realized he was made just, or "righteous," only because God's grace and sheer mercy justified him through his faith and nothing else. As Luther described it, "I felt I had been born anew and that the gates of heaven had been opened."[6]

That did it for Martin Luther, and he went on to touch off the Protestant Reformation.[7] He realized that the gospel invited him to faith in and commitment to a person—Jesus Christ. *That* is what saves, and that, as we shall see, is what the book of Romans is all about.

FOR FURTHER THOUGHT

1. Take a sheet of paper and write your definition of "the gospel." What does the good news mean to you personally? Can you list three to six ways the gospel affects your life?

2. Memorize Romans 1:16. Then do a study of the word "salvation" by summarizing the following Bible verses: Psalm 37:39; John 1:9; Acts 4:12; 15:11; Galatians 1:3-4; 2 Timothy 1:8-9; 1 Thessalonians 5:9-10.

3. Compare Ephesians 2:8-10 with Titus 3:4-7. What part do "works" play in the Christian's life? See also James 2:14-19.

4. Martin Luther, leader of the Protestant Reformation, said, "Whatever your heart clings to and relies on is your God." Do you agree with this statement? Why or why not?

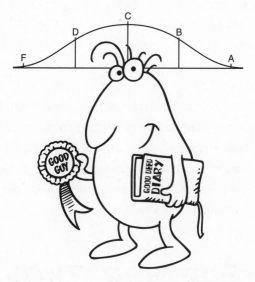

CHAPTER 2

Does God Ever Grade on a Curve?

"Grading on a curve" is a familiar term to the high school or college student. The teacher takes all the scores and lists them from highest to lowest. Then he plots a "curve" that finds some students falling in the A category, others in B, many in the C range, and the lower scores fall into D and F positions. Does God grade men this way? A lot of people talk like they think so: "Well, I'm not half as bad as . . . I live a pretty good life. I never steal or cheat . . . Why, I don't even kick my dog . . ."

Surely God, in His benevolent love and kindness, will give a passing grade and heavenly diploma to people who "do their best"? Let us see what Paul says.

ROMANS 1:18-32

[18]But God shows his anger from heaven against all sinful, wicked people who push the truth away from themselves. [19]For the truth about God is known to them instinctively. God has put this knowledge in their hearts. [20]From the time the world was created, people have seen the earth and sky and all that God made. They can clearly see his invisible qualities—his eternal power and divine nature. So they have no excuse whatsoever for not knowing God. [21]Yes, they knew God, but they wouldn't worship him as God or even give him thanks. And they began to think up foolish ideas of what God was like. The result was that their minds became dark and confused. [22]Claiming to be wise, they became utter fools instead. [23]And instead of worshiping the glorious, ever-living God, they worshiped idols made to look like mere people, or birds and animals and snakes.

[24]So God let them go ahead and do whatever shameful things their hearts desired. As a result, they did vile and degrading things with each other's bodies. [25]Instead of believing what they knew was the truth about God, they deliberately chose to believe lies. So they worshiped the things God made but not the Creator himself, who is to be praised forever. Amen.

[26]That is why God abandoned them to their shameful desires. Even the women turned against the natural

way to have sex and instead indulged in sex with each other. [27]And the men, instead of having normal sexual relationships with women, burned with lust for each other. Men did shameful things with other men and, as a result, suffered within themselves the penalty they so richly deserved.

[28]When they refused to acknowledge God, he abandoned them to their evil minds and let them do things that should never be done. [29]Their lives became full of every kind of wickedness, sin, greed, hate, envy, murder, fighting, deception, malicious behavior, and gossip. [30]They are backstabbers, haters of God, insolent, proud, and boastful. They are forever inventing new ways of sinning and are disobedient to their parents. [31]They refuse to understand, break their promises, and are heartless and unforgiving. [32]They are fully aware of God's death penalty for those who do these things, yet they go right ahead and do them anyway. And, worse yet, they encourage others to do them, too.

THOSE PAGAN "BAD GUYS"

What have we here? What a degrading view of humanity. This sounds like a description of the "bad guys," those pagans who have deliberately chosen to push away God's truth.

Note that Paul, however, doesn't leave any of these "bad guys" with an excuse. He plainly states that man can know his creator. Man can see all about him in creation the handiwork of God (see Rom. 1:20). But instead of acknowledging God, worshiping Him and thanking Him, these pagan reprobates turn from God to themselves. They think up silly ideas of what God is like (see v. 23). They turn from the light and live more and more among the shadows. Look at the list of offenses: murder, fornication, adultery, homosexuality, greed, hate, envy, lying, etc. (see vv. 24-32). Although Paul wrote this during the first century, it is an accurate description for our world today. Men and women have rebelled against God and this is the result: Their selfishness corrupts everything they touch. They see no need to turn to God. What right does God have to interfere with their lives? They will do as they please and be their own boss.

And note verse 32: Even though they know of God's death penalty for all these crimes, they go right ahead and do them anyway—and even urge others to get in on all the fun. They have drifted so far from God that they no longer see or care about the consequences of their actions.

"Well," you may be thinking. "I'm glad that's over. I'm not like that. Those people need the gospel, but I fail to see what this has to do with me."

You're not like this? You try to live right? Read on.

ROMANS 2:1-16

¹You may be saying, "What terrible people you have been talking about!" But you are just as bad, and you have no excuse! When you say they are wicked and should be punished, you are condemning yourself, for you do these very same things. ²And we know that God, in his justice, will punish anyone who does such things. ³Do you think that God will judge and condemn others for doing them and not judge you when you do them, too? ⁴Don't you realize how kind, tolerant, and patient God is with you? Or don't you care? Can't you see how kind he has been in giving you time to turn from your sin?

⁵But no, you won't listen. So you are storing up terrible punishment for yourself because of your stubborn-

ness in refusing to turn from your sin. For there is going to come a day of judgment when God, the just judge of all the world, [6]will judge all people according to what they have done. [7]He will give eternal life to those who persist in doing what is good, seeking after the glory and honor and immortality that God offers. [8]But he will pour out his anger and wrath on those who live for themselves, who refuse to obey the truth and practice evil deeds. [9]There will be trouble and calamity for everyone who keeps on sinning—for the Jew first and also for the Gentile. [10]But there will be glory and honor and peace from God for all who do good—for the Jew first and also for the Gentile. [11]For God does not show favoritism.

[12]God will punish the Gentiles when they sin, even though they never had God's written law. And he will punish the Jews when they sin, for they do have the law. [13]For it is not merely knowing the law that brings God's approval. Those who obey the law will be declared right in God's sight. [14]Even when Gentiles, who do not have God's written law, instinctively follow what the law says, they show that in their hearts they know right from wrong. [15]They demonstrate that God's law is written within them, for their own consciences either accuse them or tell them they are doing what is right. [16]The day will surely come when God, by Jesus Christ, will judge everyone's secret life. This is my message.

WE ALL HAVE SOME DIRTY CLOSETS

Now wait just a minute. Is Paul being fair when he says that you are "just as bad" as the pagans? What does he mean?

It means Paul is turning his attention to the good, moral folks who don't realize they also have a problem called "sin." It's easy for "moral" people to think only of their own goodness and fail to look into their hearts. They think of how "nice" they are without realizing that they, too, are under God's judgment. It's an old story. We may see sin in someone else, but we often fail to see similar sins in ourselves. We can point out another's hatred but cannot recognize our own envy. We think someone else has a lot of nerve to be bragging all the time, yet we fail to detect pride within ourselves. It's easy to fall into the trap of thinking that goodness on the outside—acts of tolerance and righteousness—will win God's approval and a passing grade, but God doesn't grade on a curve.

Reading between the lines, we can imagine that Paul is thinking about himself as he writes. Before Paul had his life-changing encounter with Christ, he was an "ethical" person who looked down his nose at a bad world. But when he met Christ, Paul began to see himself as he really was on the inside. Then he realized he was no longer blameless.

This can only happen when Christ confronts us. It only happens when we view ourselves in His light. As long as we compare ourselves with others, we think we're pretty good. But when we come into the presence of His perfection, that's a different story.

Our secret lives are laid open before God. And that's tough to take. We wouldn't want other people to know these things about us. We try to appear good before others, to keep up a front. But no matter how well we may think we are fooling them, inside we all have some dirty closets that we don't want anybody to discover. In fact, we've locked the doors and thrown away the keys.

God knows all about that. *Nothing* is hidden from His sight. And therefore these words of judgment and punishment are spoken to convict everyone of his or her need for Christ. *Everyone* needs the gospel. The pagan "bad guy," the moral "good guy" . . . and, yes, Paul even has a few words for the "religious" ones, in fact the most religious ones of all—the Jews. And Paul should know. He was once a "religious Jew" himself, and here is what he says.

ROMANS 2:17-29

[17]If you are a Jew, you are relying on God's law for your special relationship with him. You boast that all is well between yourself and God. [18]Yes, you know what he wants; you know right from wrong because you have been taught his law. [19]You are convinced that you are a guide for the blind and a beacon light for people who are lost in darkness without God. [20]You think you can instruct the ignorant and teach children the ways of God. For you are certain that in God's law you have complete knowledge and truth.

[21]Well then, if you teach others, why don't you teach yourself? You tell others not to steal, but do you steal? [22]You say it is wrong to commit adultery, but do you do it? You condemn idolatry, but do you steal from pagan temples? [23]You are so proud of knowing the law, but you dishonor God by breaking it. [24]No wonder the Scriptures say, "The world blasphemes the name of God because of you."

[25]The Jewish ceremony of circumcision is worth something only if you obey God's law. But if you don't obey God's law, you are no better off than an uncircumcised Gentile. [26]And if the Gentiles obey God's law, won't God give them all the rights and honors of being his own people? [27]In fact, uncircumcised Gentiles who keep God's law will be much better off than you Jews who are circumcised and know so much about God's law but don't obey it.

[28]For you are not a true Jew just because you were born of Jewish parents or because you have gone through the Jewish ceremony of circumcision. [29]No, a true Jew is one whose heart is right with God. And true circumcision is not a cutting of the body but a change of heart produced by God's Spirit. Whoever has that kind of change seeks praise from God, not from people.

THE WORLD HATES GOD BECAUSE OF YOUR RELIGION

Paul speaks to the Jews of his time. They were religious. They read their Bible regularly. They prayed, fasted, tithed and worshiped God. They were the good, solidly religious people who never questioned their standing with God. It never crossed their minds that they too might be under God's condemnation, but they were.

What had gone wrong? Paul knew. The Jews had grown proud, and their pride had let to hypocrisy. They were proud of knowing God's laws, but they dishonored Him by breaking them (see Rom. 2:23)! Paul even adds this accusation in verse 24: "No wonder the Scriptures say, 'The world blasphemes the name of God because of you!'"[1]

And the same thing happens today. In many churches, religion comes before personal commitment to Christ. Religion can make you proud and self-righteous, but in reality you fail to be kind, honest, humble and loving. Why do so many people stay away from the church? Why do they accuse Christians of hypocrisy? Because they see through the game called "religion," and they call it phony.

Let's be honest about this. It just isn't a case of "sinners who don't want to see the light." True, the devil is blinding them (see

2 Cor. 4:4), but religious hypocrisy in the Church isn't making things any clearer.

Paul exposes the failure of "religion" in this passage. He flatly states that no one is free from sin. Even religious people, even the chosen Jews, need a change of mind and heart. That's the only thing that counts.

It's fairly obvious by now that God doesn't grade on any kind of curve. In fact, all of us fail to get a passing grade. And so Paul sums up God's case against mankind with this final indictment:

ROMANS 3:1-20

[1]Then what's the advantage of being a Jew? Is there any value in the Jewish ceremony of circumcision? [2]Yes, being a Jew has many advantages. First of all, the Jews were entrusted with the whole revelation of God.

[3]True, some of them were unfaithful; but just because they broke their promises, does that mean God will break his promises? [4]Of course not! Though everyone else in the world is a liar, God is true. As the Scriptures say, "He will be proved right in what he says, and he will win his case in court."

[5]"But," some say, "our sins serve a good purpose, for people will see God's goodness when he declares us sinners to be innocent. Isn't it unfair, then, for God to punish us?" (That is actually the way some people talk.) [6]Of course not! If God is not just, how is he qualified to judge the world? [7]"But," some might still argue, "how can God judge and condemn me as a sinner if my dishonesty highlights his truthfulness and brings him more glory?" [8]If you follow that kind of thinking, however, you might as well say that the more we sin the

...EVEN THE "RELIGIOUS" PERSON CAN'T REACH HIGH ENOUGH TO MEET GOD'S STANDARD— A CHANGED MIND AND HEART.

better it is! Those who say such things deserve to be condemned, yet some slander me by saying this is what I preach!

⁹Well then, are we Jews better than others? No, not at all, for we have already shown that all people, whether Jews or Gentiles, are under the power of sin. ¹⁰As the Scriptures say,

> No one is good—not even one. ¹¹No one has real understanding; no one is seeking God. ¹²All have turned away from God; all have gone wrong. No one does good, not even one. ¹³Their talk is foul, like the stench from an open grave. Their speech is filled with lies. The poison of a deadly snake drips from their lips. ¹⁴Their mouths are full of cursing and bitterness. ¹⁵They are quick to commit murder. ¹⁶Wherever they go, destruction and misery follow them. ¹⁷They do not know what true peace is. ¹⁸They have no fear of God to restrain them.

¹⁹Obviously, the law applies to those to whom it was given, for its purpose is to keep people from having excuses and to bring the entire world into judgment before God. ²⁰For no one can ever be made right in God's sight by doing what his law commands. For the more we know God's law, the clearer it becomes that we aren't obeying it.

NOBODY BATS A THOUSAND

So there you are. This is hardly the way *we* would normally evaluate humanity, but this is *God's* evaluation of us.

NOBODY BATS 1.000

PAGAN   MORAL   RELIGIOUS

Let's sum it all up in baseball language. There are all kinds of ballplayers in the major leagues. There is the poor player who has a .180 batting average. There is the good player who hits .285. And then there is the batting champ who comes up with an amazing .374. But who bats 1.000? No one—from Babe Ruth to Barry Bonds—no one bats 1.000.

God looks at man and sees him stepping up to the plate, grounding out and striking out time and again, even though once in a while he manages to get a double off the boards. Even for the best of us, it's a pretty poor performance. No one bats 1.000.

Therefore the good news is not only for the "bad guys" who don't measure up. It's for the "good guys" who think they measure up, and for the "religious" who are trying to measure up. How then does the good news work? If all of us stand condemned, how can anyone get off the hook? Paul will spell that out next.

FOR FURTHER THOUGHT

1. Write down your own definition of "sin." Do you think some sins are worse than others? Why? Does Paul seem to think some sins are worse than others?

2. Summarize what these verses say about sin: Genesis 4:7; 1 Kings 8:46; Proverbs 20:9; Isaiah 53:6; James 4:17; 1 John 1:8; 3:4.

3. Read Romans 1:18. What does "pushing away the truth" have to do with sin?

4. Major Andrian Mikolayev, Russian cosmonaut, said that while he was in orbit he "didn't see God up there." Astronaut Gordon Cooper, who also flew in several space missions, responded by saying, "I didn't see God either, but I saw many of the wonders He created." Read Romans 1:19-20. What would you say to the person who claims, "There is no God because I can't see Him"?

CHAPTER 3

Are Christians on Parole or Fully Pardoned?

Seems like a strange way to put it: parole or pardon for the Christian? But think about it. When a prisoner is pardoned, he is free unconditionally, no strings or red tape attached. But when a man is paroled, there are conditions. He still has to report to his parole officer. He can't go here; he can't go there. He can't do this; he can't do that. Are you getting the point? A lot of Christians live like they are on parole, act like they're on parole and talk like they're on parole. But has *God* put the Christian on parole? Paul's next few lines are some of his most profound, for here in a few bold strokes of the pen is the heart of the good news.

ROMANS 3:21-31

[21]But now God has shown us a different way of being right in his sight—not by obeying the law but by the way promised in the Scriptures long ago. [22]We are made right in God's sight when we trust in Jesus Christ to take away our sins. And we all can be saved in this same way, no matter who we are or what we have done.

[23]For all have sinned; all fall short of God's glorious standard. [24]Yet now God in his gracious kindness declares us not guilty. He has done this through Christ Jesus, who has freed us by taking away our sins. [25]For God sent Jesus to take the punishment for our sins and to satisfy God's anger against us. We are made right with God when we believe that Jesus shed his blood, sacrificing his life for us. God was being entirely fair and just when he did not punish those who sinned in former times. [26]And he is entirely fair and just in this present time when he declares sinners to be right in his sight because they believe in Jesus.

[27]Can we boast, then, that we have done anything to be accepted by God? No, because our acquittal is not based on our good deeds. It is based on our faith. [28]So we are made right with God through faith and not by obeying the law.

[29]After all, God is not the God of the Jews only, is he? Isn't he also the God of the Gentiles? Of course he is. [30]There is only one God, and there is only one way of being accepted by him. He makes people right with himself only by faith, whether they are Jews or Gentiles.

³¹Well then, if we emphasize faith, does this mean that we can forget about the law? Of course not! In fact, only when we have faith do we truly fulfill the law.

THERE IS NOTHING YOU CAN DO, EXCEPT...

Now we have come to the vital answer Christianity offers to all who have sinned and fallen short (see Rom. 3:23): God has provided for our salvation. He came into the world in the person of Jesus Christ and suffered for us on a bloody and terrible cross. God allowed His only Son to take our sin upon Himself so that we could be "justified." Justified?

The key statements in this section of Romans is verse 24. The *New King James Version* puts it this way: "Being justified freely by His grace through the redemption that is in Christ Jesus." There are three words in this powerful little verse that are worth a bit of further study: "justified," "grace" and "redemption."

Justified

To be "justified" before God means that God's justice has been satisfied through the substitutionary death of His Son, Jesus Christ. Christ paid the penalty for our sin, and He also removed the guilt for our sin. This last point regarding guilt is an important fact that many Christians overlook (or never really understand).

For example, you can try to illustrate justification with a traffic ticket. Suppose you have to go to court for speeding. But you do not wind up paying the fine. You learn that it has been paid by someone else—possibly good old Dad or rich Uncle Charley. Getting your fine paid by someone else partially explains justification, but God goes one step further. While the person with a traffic ticket might get his fine paid, it doesn't alter the fact that he is guilty. But when the sinner turns to God through Christ, *his guilt is wiped out along with the penalty!*

In God's eyes, the Christian is completely pardoned for all past sins. God declares us not guilty of having offended Him if we trust in Jesus Christ (see Rom. 3:24). But there's more. God not only pardons us, He also makes us one of the family so to speak—each of us becomes a spiritual son or daughter and heir (see John 1:12; Rom. 8:16). The Christian can't completely understand this, but he or she can say, "God looks on me just as if I'd never sinned."

How and why can this be? The next keyword is the clue.

Grace

We are justified freely by God's *grace*—His unmerited favor, mercy and love. Again, like justification, you can only *try* to illustrate grace.

Grace is like getting two more days to complete an assignment, even though you've goofed off for six weeks and missed the deadline.

Grace is like getting a warning from the traffic officer, instead of a $200 fine and suspended license.

Grace is like being able to retrieve files you accidentally deleted, even when the techs say they're gone forever.

Grace is getting another chance, even though you haven't earned it or deserved it. (You may not even want it!)

But no earthly analogy really explains God's grace. God's unmerited love and mercy are available to everyone, *even those who hate Him*. When we are truly sorry for our sins, and when we trust Christ to be our personal Savior from sin, God freely forgives and accepts us, no matter what we have done. Only God could offer grace like that!

There is one more "rather important" point.

Redemption

We are justified freely by God's grace through the *redemption* that is in Christ Jesus. Redemption involves payment. Redemption means "releasing from bondage by payment of a price." The idea of a ransom is involved.

Do you remember some of the huge ransoms paid to kidnappers? The Lindberghs paid $50,000 in an effort to save their son. The Weyerhausers, timber tycoons in the state of Washington, paid $200,000 for the release of their nine-year-old boy. Frank Sinatra paid $240,000 for the return of Frank, Jr. Recently, a book was released describing the rise in international kidnappings, with reports of as many as 20,000 to 30,000 people being taken hostage each year.[1] It has been claimed that these kidnappers have received as much as a $50 million ransom to release their hostages.[2]

But Christ did more than pay a sum of money for our lives. He gave His own life as a ransom to deliver us from the bondage of sin (see Mark 10:45).

Mankind is separated from God—lost. We are sinners. We are captives in the hands of the devil. Jesus came and died to pay the maximum price to buy us back, for we are rightfully His. The price was *His own life*, given on the cross. He purchased us not with silver or gold but with His own blood (see Acts 20:28).

So what is there left for us to do?

Nothing.

Nothing except to receive God's good news, believe it, have faith. "Because our acquittal is not based on our good deeds. It is based on our faith" (Rom. 3:27). Faith in Christ changes us and makes us new persons. Faith, as Martin Luther put it, "is a living, daring confidence in God's grace, so sure and certain that a man would stake his life on it a thousand times."

There is no magic in faith. Faith is simply our response to the salvation Christ obtained for us. We now face God unafraid.

The penalty and guilt of sin are gone, paid for by God Himself. Religious rites and works do not make us right with God—and God doesn't expect them after we come to Christ. We are *fully pardoned*, even our guilt is gone. We are not "on parole," earning our freedom, continuing to pay the debts for our crimes.

"Wait a minute," you say. "Does that mean I can live any way I want to and not be concerned about obeying God's laws?" As *The Living Bible* puts it: "Just the opposite!" (v. 31). Being pardoned by God makes you a new person. You trust Christ for power to live as you should each day. "In fact, only when we trust Jesus can we truly obey him" (v. 31, *TLB*). You can't trust Christ by "being religious." Trusting and religious self-effort are contradictory. To trust Christ is to be a Christian *without* being religious.

You see, God has always saved by faith. Before the Law given through Moses, God called a man named Abraham. He became the father of the Jewish people. God sought out this Abraham, who lived almost 2,000 years before Christ, and he responded *by faith*.

ROMANS 4:1-25

[1]Abraham was, humanly speaking, the founder of our Jewish nation. What were his experiences concerning this question of being saved by faith? [2]Was it because of his good deeds that God accepted him? If so, he would have had something to boast about. But from God's point of view Abraham had no basis at all for pride. [3]For the Scriptures tell us, "Abraham believed God, so God declared him to be righteous."

[4]When people work, their wages are not a gift. Workers earn what they receive. [5]But people are declared

righteous because of their faith, not because of their work.

[6]King David spoke of this, describing the happiness of an undeserving sinner who is declared to be righteous: [7]"Oh, what joy for those whose disobedience is forgiven, whose sins are put out of sight. [8]Yes, what joy for those whose sin is no longer counted against them by the Lord."

[9]Now then, is this blessing only for the Jews, or is it for Gentiles, too? Well, what about Abraham? We have been saying he was declared righteous by God because of his faith. [10]But how did his faith help him? Was he declared righteous only after he had been circumcised, or was it before he was circumcised? The answer is that God accepted him first, and then he was circumcised later!

[11]The circumcision ceremony was a sign that Abraham already had faith and that God had already accepted him and declared him to be righteous—even before he was circumcised. So Abraham is the spiritual father of those who have faith but have not been circumcised. They are made right with God by faith. [12]And Abraham is also the spiritual father of those who have been circumcised, but only if they have the same kind of faith Abraham had before he was circumcised.

[13]It is clear, then, that God's promise to give the whole earth to Abraham and his descendants was not based on obedience to God's law, but on the new relationship with God that comes by faith. [14]So if you claim that God's promise is for those who obey God's law and think they are "good enough" in God's sight, then you are saying that faith is useless. And in that case, the promise is also meaningless. [15]But the law

brings punishment on those who try to obey it. (The only way to avoid breaking the law is to have no law to break!)

[16]So that's why faith is the key! God's promise is given to us as a free gift. And we are certain to receive it, whether or not we follow Jewish customs, if we have faith like Abraham's. For Abraham is the father of all who believe. [17]That is what the Scriptures mean when God told him, "I have made you the father of many nations." This happened because Abraham believed in the God who brings the dead back to life and who brings into existence what didn't exist before.

[18]When God promised Abraham that he would become the father of many nations, Abraham believed him. God had also said, "Your descendants will be as numerous as the stars," even though such a promise seemed utterly impossible! [19]And Abraham's faith did not weaken, even though he knew that he was too old to be a father at the age of one hundred and that Sarah, his wife, had never been able to have children.

[20]Abraham never wavered in believing God's promise. In fact, his faith grew stronger, and in this he brought glory to God. [21]He was absolutely convinced that God was able to do anything he promised. [22]And because of Abraham's faith, God declared him to be righteous.

[23]Now this wonderful truth—that God declared him to be righteous—wasn't just for Abraham's benefit. [24]It was for us, too, assuring us that God will also declare us to be righteous if we believe in God, who brought Jesus our Lord back from the dead. [25]He was handed over to die because of our sins, and he was raised from the dead to make us right with God.

THE FAITH YOU HAVE IS THE FAITH YOU SHOW

Why does Paul stop to talk about Abraham? He has good reason. He is writing to Jews and Gentiles who have become Christians. He has made the claim that faith is central to being justified before God. But what if this faith idea is not in harmony with God's revealed will in the Old Testament? If there is no biblical foundation for the importance of faith, then the Jews could claim Paul to be a heretic. If it is possible to be justified by works, to be saved by keeping God's law, then Christianity is wrong.

Paul doesn't choose Abraham as an example by accident. Abraham was the father of the Jewish nation (see Gen. 17:1-8). If Paul can show that Abraham, of all people, was justified by faith and not by his works, he has made his point: The Christian faith is firmly rooted in the Bible, the Old Testament.

And Paul does make his point. Look again at Romans 4:1-5. Abraham believed God and that is why God forgave his sins and declared him just and righteous.[3]

In Romans 4, Paul tells us to read the story of Abraham and decide for ourselves. Abraham was called by God to leave his home and go to a new land to found the Jewish nation. He *went*. He was told that his wife would have a child, even though he and his wife were well past the age for having children. But *he believed*, and Sarah did bear a son.

With Abraham it was all faith. He believed God. He obeyed God. He had faith and he acted on it. He did not simply sit back and do nothing. Faith is response, action. Belief (mental assent) may be for the study, but faith is for the road.

Abraham is a prime example. The faith you have is the faith you show. Faith is not merely knowing what you believe. Faith is life lived in a new way—in response to God's revealed will.

Faith is practical. Faith is not fantasy. Faith means risk. Abraham went out, not knowing where he was going.

Consider these famous words spoken by Neil Armstrong when he stepped out of that lunar module and touched the surface of the moon for the first time: "That's one small step for man—one giant leap for mankind."[4] Careful calculations made the astronauts believe that things would work out and they blasted off. But Abraham had even greater faith. *He had no way of calculating how things would work out.* He accepted God's Word. He stepped out in trust and obedience. The faith you have is the faith you show. And when you have faith, it does show, as you'll see in the next chapter.

FOR FURTHER THOUGHT

1. Read Romans 3:23-26 in different Bible translations. (Note that Romans 3:23-24 is one thought, and verses 23 and 24 should be read together.) Compare Romans 3:23 with Ephesians 1:7; Colossians 1:14; Hebrews 9:12-15. Describe in your own words the importance of the blood of Christ to a Christian's salvation.

2. Memorize Romans 3:24. Meditate on 2 Corinthians 12:9; Philippians 4:19 and Titus 3:5. Write a brief statement of what God's grace means to you.

3. Read Acts 13:39 and Galatians 3:24. Write them out in your own words, and then write a definition of "justification by grace."

4. Compare Galatians 3:13; Colossians 1:13-14; Hebrews 9:11-12; 1 Peter 1:18-19. Write out a definition of "redemption" and then compare it with a dictionary's definition. How does being redeemed inspire you to step out in faith and obey God?

Is Your Faith More Than "Fire Insurance"?

Being saved—justified by faith in Christ—assures us of eternal life. But is that the whole story? A criticism of Christianity is that it just offers "pie in the sky by and by." Christians are accused—and some with good reason—that they get saved in order to take out a "fire insurance policy" against going to hell. But their lives don't reflect any true change of heart. What about this? Does being a Christian provide benefits and results for this life—*right now*?

ROMANS 5:1-11

[1]Therefore, since we have been made right in God's sight by faith, we have peace with God because of what Jesus Christ our Lord has done for us. [2]Because of our faith, Christ has brought us into this place of highest privilege where we now stand, and we confidently and joyfully look forward to sharing God's glory.

[3]We can rejoice, too, when we run into problems and trials, for we know that they are good for us—they help us learn to endure. [4]And endurance develops strength of character in us, and character strengthens our confident expectation of salvation. [5]And this expectation will not disappoint us. For we know how dearly God loves us, because he has given us the Holy Spirit to fill our hearts with his love.

[6]When we were utterly helpless, Christ came at just the right time and died for us sinners. [7]Now, no one is likely to die for a good person, though someone might be willing to die for a person who is especially good. [8]But God showed his great love for us by sending Christ to die for us while we were still sinners. [9]And since we have been made right in God's sight by the blood of Christ, he will certainly save us from God's judgment. [10]For since we were restored to friendship with God by the death of his Son while we were still his enemies, we will certainly be delivered from eternal punishment by his life. [11]So now we can rejoice in our wonderful new relationship with God—all because of what our Lord Jesus Christ has done for us in making us friends of God.

REAL FAITH BRINGS PRACTICAL RESULTS

What do most people want out of life? Confidence, peace, love, hope, happiness, security, accomplishment. They may express it in different words and ways, but their desires are pretty much the same. In the passage you have just read, Paul claims that the Christian can have all of these things. Being justified, or made right in God's sight, by faith gives us real peace with God because of what Jesus Christ our Lord has done for us (see Rom. 5:1). And, in addition, our faith brings three wonderfully practical results: We have new potential, new power and a new Friend.

New Potential

Our faith has brought us into a place of highest privilege, and we can confidently look forward to actually becoming all that God has in mind for us to be (see Rom. 5:2, *The Living Bible*).

"That sounds good," you say, "but how does it work?"

The answer is written all over Romans: Have faith, trust God, and obey Him. God is in charge; let Him call the shots. For example, in order to reach full potential, any great athlete lets the coach direct his or her training. Kurt Warner, the well-known St. Louis Rams quarterback who has used his fame as a platform for sharing his faith in Jesus, makes a clear case for listening to the coach. He says, "Coaches want someone who will listen and respond to what they are saying. Sometimes you might think the coach is wrong, but if you get on the wrong side of your coach, nothing good will come from it. Always try to do the right thing immediately. Coaches love players who get it right after being told only once what to do."[1]

New Power

Paul says that Christians can rejoice when problems come, because difficulties help them learn to endure (see Rom. 5:3). Who wants problems? Nobody, really, but problems come anyway.

Paul, however, sees a problem as something he can use, not something that lays him low. A problem gives you the opportunity to be patient, which develops strength of character. We learn to trust God more and more until our faith is really strong (see v. 4).

"All very fine," you may say, "but where is the power? Where do I get all this patience and strength? I have a short fuse and I get discouraged pretty easily at times. Sure, I start out by wanting to trust God. I even pray about my problems—passing an exam, getting that job, winning that game, making that deadline—but what happens when I don't pass, when I don't make it? What happens when there's just me and the problem?"

For the Christian it is never "just me and the problem." God is there, too. No matter what happens, we can know that all is well, that God loves us. Why? Because we can feel His love within us as the Holy Spirit fills our hearts with His love (see v. 5).

Here is the first mention of the Holy Spirit in Romans. It won't be the last. The Holy Spirit is the vital key to being a Christian without being religious. For the Christian, every trial and every problem can be a useful experience to build faith, confidence, hope, happiness—*if he or she faces it by relying on the Holy Spirit.*

How does the Christian rely on the Holy Spirit? There are various formulas, but here's one you may not have tried: *Wait. Do nothing.*

Richard Halverson, who for many years was chaplain to the United States Senate, wrote:

There are times when doing something only compounds the problem, deepens the difficulty, adds to the confusion. Doing nothing is a strategy . . . a conscious, positive, constructive strategy. Leave a glass of muddy water alone—the dirt and debris settle to the bottom. This is a way of purifying water . . . and it's a way of allowing a confused situation to clarify. Waiting brings facts into focus—helps you see them in perspective.[2]

FAITH IN CHRIST GIVES POWER TO TAKE IT WHEN THINGS GET TOUGH...

To wait doesn't mean that you never act to solve a certain problem. But to wait and do nothing in your own strength is a way to show your reliance on the Holy Spirit. Waiting, thinking and praying can give God's love, which is poured into your heart by the Holy Spirit, a chance to calm the troubled waters inside. Try it and see how it works.

New Friend

If you wanted to put one thing on the top of the "what I want out of life" heap, it would have to be love. We all want to know that we matter to someone. It can mean the difference between despair and a meaningful life.

The Christian knows that someone cares. He knows God loves him. "God showed his great love for us by sending Christ to die for us" (Rom. 5:8).

The Christian and his convictions may seem to be alone with his problems and trials. The Christian may seem small and insignificant, but he has God's Word for it that God cares. As Paul puts it, "So now we can rejoice in our wonderful new relationship with God—all because of what our Lord Jesus Christ has done for us in making us friends of God" (v. 11).

Is your faith more than fire insurance? It should be. It better be. If it isn't, perhaps you are only going through the motions—perhaps you are trying to be a Christian by being "religious."

Paul seems to digress a bit in Romans chapter 5, or is he just expanding the incredible concept of how "while we were yet sinners Christ died for us" (v. 8)? Here is profound thinking on man's sin and God's mercy.

ROMANS 5:12-21

[12]When Adam sinned, sin entered the entire human race. Adam's sin brought death, so death spread to everyone, for everyone sinned. [13]Yes, people sinned even before the law was given. And though there was no law to break, since it had not yet been given, [14]they all died anyway—even though they did not disobey an explicit commandment of God, as Adam did. What a contrast between Adam and Christ, who was yet to come! [15]And what a difference between our sin and God's generous gift of forgiveness. For this one man, Adam, brought death to many through his sin. But this other man, Jesus Christ, brought forgiveness to many through God's bountiful gift. [16]And the result of God's gracious

gift is very different from the result of that one man's sin. For Adam's sin led to condemnation, but we have the free gift of being accepted by God, even though we are guilty of many sins. [17]The sin of this one man, Adam, caused death to rule over us, but all who receive God's wonderful, gracious gift of righteousness will live in triumph over sin and death through this one man, Jesus Christ.

[18]Yes, Adam's one sin brought condemnation upon everyone, but Christ's one act of righteousness makes all people right in God's sight and gives them life. [19]Because one person disobeyed God, many people became sinners. But because one other person obeyed God, many people will be made right in God's sight.

[20]God's law was given so that all people could see how sinful they were. But as people sinned more and more, God's wonderful kindness became more abundant. [21]So just as sin ruled over all people and brought them to death, now God's wonderful kindness rules instead, giving us right standing with God and resulting in eternal life through Jesus Christ our Lord.

ADAM AND CHRIST: A WORLD OF DIFFERENCE

Scholars have written thousands of words to try to explain Romans 5:12-21, which plainly states that because Adam sinned, all the rest of us sinned, too. But that doesn't seem fair—we weren't even there. We had no part in what happened. How can Paul say that when Adam sinned, everyone sinned?

A major part of the answer lies in the fact that we are all part of the human race (what theologians call "solidarity"). As the first man, Adam was our representative and what he did affected all of us. In God's sight, we all became guilty.[3] In addition to inheriting Adam's guilt, we also inherited his sinful nature. No matter how much good human beings might do (and they do a lot), in the long run no one can entirely please God. Because of Adam's disobedience, he and all humankind after him faced death and judgment. But although one man, Adam, brought death to the world through his sin, another man, Jesus Christ, brought forgiveness through God's grace. The diagrams below sum it up:

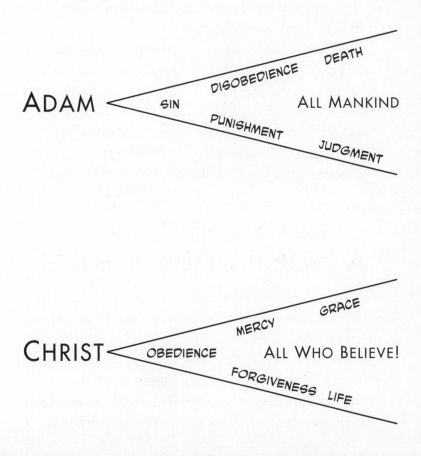

FOR FURTHER THOUGHT

1. Compare Romans 5:2 with Ephesians 3:16-21. How can you become the person God has in mind for you to be?
2. Memorize Romans 5:2. How does knowing that Christ has saved you affect your everyday life?
3. Reread Romans 5:12-21. Make a list of the ways Adam's choices affected mankind and the ways Jesus' obedience remedies them.
4. Meditate on Romans 5:21. Thank God that His wonderful kindness rules in your life and that you have right standing with Him and the promise of eternal life.

CHAPTER 5

Whose Slave Are You?

"Why, I'm not a slave to anyone. My faith makes me free!"

Why, yes, that's right—in a way. A Christian is free from the penalty for sin. In fact, he never has any more trouble with sin at all . . .

"Wait a minute; not so fast. I have plenty of trouble with sin. In fact I have more trouble with sin now that I'm a Christian than I did before."

Yes, that's right, too, and Paul had the same experience. So it is *sin in the Christian's daily life* that Paul writes about as he starts

Romans 6. He has already explained "justification by faith." Now he's going on to the subject that separates the religious striver from the trusting believer . . . sanctification. People shy away from a word like "sanctification." It sounds so formidable, so pious. What does it mean? Paul knew. In these next pages of his letter, he wrestles with the fact that a person *can't* be a growing, happy Christian by simply being religious. Mere religion, you see, is not enough.

ROMANS 6:1-23

[1]Well then, should we keep on sinning so that God can show us more and more kindness and forgiveness? [2]Of course not! Since we have died to sin, how can we continue to live in it? [3]Or have you forgotten that when we became Christians and were baptized to become one with Christ Jesus, we died with him? [4]For we died and were buried with Christ by baptism. And just as Christ was raised from the dead by the glorious power of the Father, now we also may live new lives.

[5]Since we have been united with him in his death, we will also be raised as he was. [6]Our old sinful selves were crucified with Christ so that sin might lose its power in our lives. We are no longer slaves to sin. [7]For when we died with Christ we were set free from the power of sin. [8]And since we died with Christ, we know we will also share his new life. [9]We are sure of this because Christ rose from the dead, and he will never die again. Death no longer has any power over him. [10]He died once to defeat sin, and now he lives for the glory of God. [11]So you should consider yourselves dead to sin and able to live for the glory of God through Christ Jesus.

¹²Do not let sin control the way you live; do not give in to its lustful desires. ¹³Do not let any part of your body become a tool of wickedness, to be used for sinning. Instead, give yourselves completely to God since you have been given new life. And use your whole body as a tool to do what is right for the glory of God. ¹⁴Sin is no longer your master, for you are no longer subject to the law, which enslaves you to sin. Instead, you are free by God's grace.

¹⁵So since God's grace has set us free from the law, does this mean we can go on sinning? Of course not! ¹⁶Don't you realize that whatever you choose to obey becomes your master? You can choose sin, which leads to death, or you can choose to obey God and receive his approval. ¹⁷Thank God! Once you were slaves of sin, but now you have obeyed with all your heart the new teaching God has given you. ¹⁸Now you are free from sin, your old master, and you have become slaves to your new master, righteousness.

¹⁹I speak this way, using the illustration of slaves and masters, because it is easy to understand. Before, you let yourselves be slaves of impurity and lawlessness. Now you must choose to be slaves of righteousness so that you will become holy.

²⁰In those days, when you were slaves of sin, you weren't concerned with doing what was right. ²¹And what was the result? It was not good, since now you are ashamed of the things you used to do, things that end in eternal doom. ²²But now you are free from the power of sin and have become slaves of God. Now you do those things that lead to holiness and result in eternal life. ²³For the wages of sin is death, but the free gift of God is eternal life through Christ Jesus our Lord.

You Belong to Your Choice

"Well, I can't be perfect anyway. So what if I sin a little? God will forgive me."

Ever get an idea like that? It's a typical trap for any Christian, for as any Christian knows, "getting saved" doesn't solve all your problems with sin. You are saved from the *penalty* and *guilt* of sin—"justified by faith" as Paul explained it in Romans 3 and 4. But the *power* of sin is still there, working on you and tempting you. The natural conclusion, then, is to let the "slips befall you where they may." There is always 1 John 1:9. Confess. God is faithful. He forgives and cleanses. And soon it becomes a kind of game, but you never win, and you don't feel right about it.

Paul deals briefly with this idea of "let's sin all the more, so God can show all the more grace and mercy." He says, "God forbid!" And then he comes up with more good news about the Good News of Jesus. We don't have to keep on sinning, because sin's power over us was broken when we became Christians.

Sin's power broken? It doesn't seem that way. Why do Christians still have so many temptations? And why do they still sin?

Paul sails into some deep waters in Romans 6. He is drawing pictures with words, symbolizing what happens when a person becomes a Christian. The Christian becomes a part of Christ, and so the Christian figuratively "dies" with Christ as He died on the cross. And the Christian also rises with Christ just as He rose from the grave.

Hard to understand? Yes, but this is another vital key to the difference between "religion" and Christianity. A Christian is not someone who simply follows Christ's great teachings. A Christian is one who is *one with Christ* in a *personal* relationship. That is why Paul says in verse 6: "Our old sinful selves were crucified with Christ so that sin might lose its power in our lives. We are no longer slaves to sin."

"My evil desires were nailed to the cross? That part of me that loves to sin was fatally wounded? It doesn't seem that way to me . . ."

Perhaps it doesn't. But the key to this passage is to remember that Paul is painting a picture, and *it's the way you want to look at that picture that makes the difference.*

So, look at it this way. Paul is saying that becoming a Christian means that you will not only start to follow Christ but that *you also identify with Him—you become part of Him.* And just as Christ conquered the power of sin with His death and resurrection, Christ also struck a telling blow against the old, sinful nature that is part of every one of us.

The question is, do you want to let that telling blow work in your favor or do you want to still fight your own battles? This is the paradox. Christ doesn't force His way into your life. He doesn't walk in and say, "I'm taking over. From now on you do things my way, or else." He gives you a choice. You are no longer under sin's complete domination, but neither are you a robot. (Robots don't get tempted, but they don't experience love, joy, peace and satisfaction either.)

So Paul says that we should "reckon" (look upon) our old sinful nature as dead. In other words, we *really believe* that "sin's fangs have been pulled" and that we are alive to God, alert to Him, through Jesus Christ our Lord.

Paul never claims that the Christian is free from temptation, impervious to sin, sealed in a plastic coating called salvation. Temptations still come, but what Paul means is that *now you don't have sin as your only alternative.* Another route is open—obedience to Christ. The choice is yours.

Choice is always a part of life. And with every choice you make, you are actually turning toward sin or toward Christ.

There is no middle ground. You do not remain the same. You are always changing.

And you become like the one you obey. If you serve sin, it means frustration, disillusionment, a kind of cynical hardening toward the gospel. But if you serve Christ, He molds your life. The one to whom you offer yourself will take you and be your master, and you will be his slave. *And you become like the one to whom you belong!*

And so we choose one of two masters. We serve God or sin. Some think that while they may "sin a little," they are still master of a particular habit or practice. It doesn't work out that way. You don't master a sin; it masters you. *You belong to the power you choose to obey.* You accept Christ by faith; but unless your faith in Him is constant and real, sin will still rule your life.

You see, there are three aspects to sanctification: positional, experiential and ultimate.

Positional sanctification means every believer is "sanctified" in the sense that he or she enjoys the benefit of God's accomplished work through salvation. Our position is that we have a relationship with God by being one with Christ.[1] Paul even said those who were living in carnal sin in the church at Corinth were sanctified and set apart by God because of what Christ had done for them (see 1 Cor. 6:11).

Ultimate sanctification refers to heaven, our eternal life with Christ. It is another term for glorification, that is, being like Christ at His coming (see 1 John 3:1-3).

But what Paul is directly concerned with in Romans 6 is experiential sanctification, actually experiencing triumph over sin in your daily life.

We can define "sanctification" in neat theological terms: "Being set apart for use by God through holy living in accordance with His will."[2] But perhaps this ponderous word has more meaning when seen simply as: "Letting Christ make a real difference in your life." And the only way there can be a real difference is being able to freely choose your own master. Without the element of choice, your sanctification would be a sterile, mechanical procedure. You would be a "justified computer." But God doesn't want computers. He wants Christians who see themselves as dead to sin and alive to Him, through Jesus Christ.

Whose slave are you? Go back to Romans 6:11. *It all depends on how you choose to look at living the Christian life.* "Being religious" doesn't help here. You are a part of Christ, but you have a choice: sin or obedience to Him. *You belong to your choice.*

Paul isn't through with showing us that the Christian life is a personal relationship with Christ. In Romans 7:1-14, he uses marriage to illustrate the bond between the Christian and his or her Lord. The Christian is no longer married to the law because he or she has died to sin and dissolved that contract. The Christian is now married, so to speak, to Christ.

ROMANS 7:1-14

[1]Now, dear brothers and sisters—you who are familiar with the law—don't you know that the law applies only to a person who is still living? [2]Let me illustrate. When a woman marries, the law binds her to her husband as long as he is alive. But if he dies, the laws of marriage no longer apply to her. [3]So while her husband is alive, she would be committing adultery if she married another man. But if her husband dies, she is free from that law and does not commit adultery when she remarries.

[4]So this is the point: The law no longer holds you in its power, because you died to its power when you died with Christ on the cross. And now you are united with

the one who was raised from the dead. As a result, you can produce good fruit, that is, good deeds for God. [5]When we were controlled by our old nature, sinful desires were at work within us, and the law aroused these evil desires that produced sinful deeds, resulting in death. [6]But now we have been released from the law, for we died with Christ, and we are no longer captive to its power. Now we can really serve God, not in the old way by obeying the letter of the law, but in the new way, by the Spirit.

[7]Well then, am I suggesting that the law of God is evil? Of course not! The law is not sinful, but it was the law that showed me my sin. I would never have known that coveting is wrong if the law had not said, "Do not covet." [8]But sin took advantage of this law and aroused all kinds of forbidden desires within me! If there were no law, sin would not have that power.

[9]I felt fine when I did not understand what the law demanded. But when I learned the truth, I realized I had broken the law and was a sinner, doomed to die. [10]So the good law, which was supposed to show me the way of life, instead gave me the death penalty. [11]Sin took advantage of the law and fooled me; it took the good law and used it to make me guilty of death. [12]But still, the law itself is holy and right and good.

[13]But how can that be? Did the law, which is good, cause my doom? Of course not! Sin used what was good to bring about my condemnation. So we can see how terrible sin really is. It uses God's good commandment for its own evil purposes.

[14]The law is good, then. The trouble is not with the law but with me, because I am sold into slavery, with sin as my master.

THE PROBLEM IS NOT
WITH THE LAW

Paul wants to clarify an important point right here. He opens
up by saying that the Christian is no longer married to the law.
He has "died" as far as the law is concerned and is now one with
Christ. But Paul doesn't want you to get the idea that the Law
is something evil. The real enemy is sin—damnable stuff that
uses God's good laws for its own evil purposes.

Paul knows that the trouble is not in the law; the trouble is
in him, as he will show in the next part of his letter.

FOR FURTHER THOUGHT

1. Compare Romans 6:1-11 with Ephesians 4:20-32 and
   Colossians 3:1-17. Write down in your own words
   what it means to be dead to sin and alive to God.

2. Review Romans 6:19-23. How do you feel about being
   a slave to God? How do you reconcile this idea with
   John 8:32?

3. Why does Christ leave the Christian with a choice
   between yielding to sin or following Him? Why doesn't
   God control the Christian so completely that sin
   would never be an issue?

4. Memorize Romans 6:16. Do you agree with this statement: You don't master a sin; it masters you? Can you
   think of any personal experiences that bear this out?

① 2 not be controlled by sin; to not give in to sinful
ways; to do what I believe would please God. To focus on
God and not self
② Its a choice know the truth b/c it frees
③ We are not robots, he wants us to want this way of life

CHAPTER 6

Spirit Versus Self: How Do I Win the War Within?

Romans 6 was "good for openers" on this problem of sin in a Christian's life, but you probably want to know a lot more. What's your problem? Temper? Impatience? Self-control? Sex? Honesty? Your thought life? Pride? Laziness? Self-centeredness? We all have our skeletons, and they don't always stay in the closet. You want to do right, but you do wrong. You want to choose obedience, but you choose sin. Sometimes you'd almost swear you were a split personality, a regular "walking civil war." Read on. Paul admits that he fights that war, too.

ROMANS 7:15-25

[15]I don't understand myself at all, for I really want to do what is right, but I don't do it. Instead, I do the very thing I hate. [16]I know perfectly well that what I am doing is wrong, and my bad conscience shows that I agree that the law is good. [17]But I can't help myself, because it is sin inside me that makes me do these evil things.

[18]I know I am rotten through and through so far as my old sinful nature is concerned. No matter which way I turn, I can't make myself do right. I want to, but I can't. [19]When I want to do good, I don't. And when I try not to do wrong, I do it anyway. [20]But if I am doing what I don't want to do, I am not really the one doing it; the sin within me is doing it.

[21]It seems to be a fact of life that when I want to do what is right, I inevitably do what is wrong. [22]I love God's law with all my heart. [23]But there is another law at work within me that is at war with my mind. This law wins the fight and makes me a slave to the sin that is still within me. [24]Oh, what a miserable person I am! Who will free me from this life that is dominated by sin? [25]Thank God! The answer is in Jesus Christ our Lord. So you see how it is: In my mind I really want to obey God's law, but because of my sinful nature I am a slave to sin.

HOW DO I GET OUT OF THIS MESS?

Does Paul's struggle sound familiar? We all experience the frustration of knowing what is right and failing to do it. This isn't supposed to be the Christian's experience, but Romans 7:15-24 draws an accurate picture of the vicious circle we all get into.

TODAY I WILL LIVE FOR CHRIST.

I start the day with devotions and feel pretty good . . .

BUT WHY DID THIS HAVE TO HAPPEN...?

But in no time at all I hit a snag, I run smack into trouble—somebody I don't like, a situation I can't handle, a nice juicy temptation . . .

I SHOULDN'T LET IT BOTHER ME... IT'S NOT A GOOD WITNESS.

I know I shouldn't let this thing get to me this way. After all, I'm supposed to act like a Christian . . .

But no matter which way I turn, or how hard I try . . .

I flub it, wind up defeated, tied in knots, a slave to sin . . .

And my question is, How do I get out of this mess? If I'm a Christian, why can't I lick this thing?

So we may as well be honest. This "new life in Christ" is no snap. We come to Christ as sinners. We are saved by God's amazing grace. We are forgiven and justified before God. *But we are still sinners after we believe.* Paul found this out. He admitted that he was "rotten through and through" (v. 18).

The inescapable fact is that by ourselves we can't do the right thing. We just don't make it. Knowing the rules, golden or otherwise, doesn't make us able to obey. We keep on falling into the trap called sin, *because we choose to.* The old nature is still in every Christian, trying to keep the new nature from taking over. And there is no "peaceful coexistence." Truly, the Christian is a "walking civil war."

Paul has the answer to winning this war. First you have to be sure you understand who is fighting it, and then you need good military strategy. Here is his battle plan.

ROMANS 8:1-17

¹So now there is no condemnation for those who belong to Christ Jesus. ²For the power of the life-giving Spirit has freed you through Christ Jesus from the power of sin that leads to death. ³The law of Moses could not save us, because of our sinful nature. But God put into effect a different plan to save us. He sent his own Son in a human body like ours, except that ours are sinful. God destroyed sin's control over us by giving his Son as a sacrifice for our sins. ⁴He did this so that the requirement of the law would be fully accomplished for us who no longer follow our sinful nature but instead follow the Spirit.

⁵Those who are dominated by the sinful nature think about sinful things, but those who are controlled

by the Holy Spirit think about things that please the Spirit. ⁶If your sinful nature controls your mind, there is death. But if the Holy Spirit controls your mind, there is life and peace. ⁷For the sinful nature is always hostile to God. It never did obey God's laws, and it never will. ⁸That's why those who are still under the control of their sinful nature can never please God.

⁹But you are not controlled by your sinful nature. You are controlled by the Spirit if you have the Spirit of God living in you. (And remember that those who do not have the Spirit of Christ living in them are not Christians at all.) ¹⁰Since Christ lives within you, even though your body will die because of sin, your spirit is alive because you have been made right with God. ¹¹The Spirit of God, who raised Jesus from the dead, lives in you. And just as he raised Christ from the dead, he will give life to your mortal body by this same Spirit living within you.

¹²So, dear brothers and sisters, you have no obligation whatsoever to do what your sinful nature urges you to do. ¹³For if you keep on following it, you will perish. But if through the power of the Holy Spirit you turn from it and its evil deeds, you will live. ¹⁴For all who are led by the Spirit of God are children of God.

¹⁵So you should not be like cowering, fearful slaves. You should behave instead like God's very own children, adopted into his family—calling him "Father, dear Father." ¹⁶For his Holy Spirit speaks to us deep in our hearts and tells us that we are God's children. ¹⁷And since we are his children, we will share his treasures—for everything God gives to his Son, Christ, is ours, too. But if we are to share his glory, we must also share his suffering.

This War Calls for Extreme Measures

So we "have the Holy Spirit." You've probably heard that before. It's a nice, comfortable, "spiritual" thought.

But what does it mean? Paul says that "the power of the life-giving Spirit" has freed us from "the power of sin that leads to death" (Rom. 8:2).

What is Paul saying? Didn't he just get through admitting that he couldn't make the grade, that he couldn't obey the law, good as the law might be? Yes, that's the point. When we try to obey the law, we are trying to do something for God. But when we follow after the Holy Spirit (see vv. 4-5), *we let God do something for us.*

Some Christians fail because they don't even know they have the Holy Spirit within them. But perhaps a lot more Christians fail because the concept of the Holy Spirit within is only that—a nice idea, a theological cliché that doesn't have a thing to do with their real lives.

But the Holy Spirit is not just a concept. He is a person. He is the Spirit of God, and He does have something to do with your life, especially if you're interested in living a Christian life, not just being "religious."

Look at it this way. If you are a Christian, you have a battle on your hands. You are constantly facing a choice between sin and obedience. The fact that you are aware of the choice, that you are concerned, shows that you want to win this war within. But how badly do you want to win it? In the 1950s and '60s the United States fought "small wars" that it didn't really try to win. Containment was more of a goal than all-out victory. A "peaceful settlement" was preferable to unconditional surrender.

You can't fight that kind of war with sin, because it will whip you every time. You have to decide which way you really want to go.

You say you "want to live for Christ . . . do the right thing . . ."

But, there's one big problem, isn't there? You are fighting this war with a reservation. You don't really want to win it, because that would mean you couldn't be in charge. But in this war, no Christian is a general. All of us are privates, and our orders are to follow after the Holy Spirit.

Paul puts the choice quite clearly in Romans 8:5: "Those who are dominated by the sinful nature think about sinful things, but those who are controlled by the Holy Spirit think about things that please the Spirit." And you know, it's a funny thing—when you wind up pleasing God, you please yourself, too. Christ conquers sin and you win that war within.

"All very true," you say. "Sounds good, but can I have a few practical instructions? Any examples you can give me of *how* to do this?"

First, get a good picture of the kind of war you're fighting. You are the battleground. The opposing forces are the Spirit and the self (human nature). "These two forces are constantly fighting each other, and your choices are never free from this conflict" (Gal. 5:17).

SELF VS. SPIRIT
FACT OF THE
CHRISTIAN LIFE.

Next, realize you don't fight this war by dashing around saying, "I'm gonna be good, I'm gonna be good. I'll think good thoughts." This is a foot-soldier war. You fight it by *walking*. And there are only two ways to walk: in the Spirit or in the flesh (going your own merry way). When Paul talks about walking and following after the Spirit, he suggests continuous action and motion. The Christian life is not simply a Sunday stroll with Jesus. It's a choice, a daily commitment to follow the Spirit—or a daily surrender to pleasing the old me, the sinful self.

For an example of walking in the Spirit, take the testimony of Nicole Johnson. When asked how her faith impacted her year touring as Miss America 2000, she replied,

[My faith] played such a tremendous role. I knew right from wrong and what was good and bad, but I needed to keep my focus on Christ. Every day was a challenge and I had to approach it as a physical battle or emotional battle, and definitely a spiritual battle. I had to pray for guidance every single moment—that God would give me the wisdom to speak at the level I needed to speak and allow me to share my testimony. I absolutely could not have made it through or accomplished the things that I was blessed enough to accomplish without Him.[1]

Exactly how was this an example of "walking in the Spirit"? Examine the situation again. Nicole prayed. (You can't walk with the Spirit and not be on speaking terms.) She asked for opportunity to show her loyalty to Christ. (You don't walk with the Spirit and deny His cause.) When the test came, she had power to meet it. (The Scriptures say that the Spirit will teach us what to say and bring it to mind when it's needed. See John 14:26.)

Nicole Johnson's success sounds fine, but you may be wondering what to do if things don't work out quite so nicely for you.

It seems more your luck to have someone say, "I understand you read the Bible and other fairy tales."

To which you brilliantly reply: "Oh, why don't you drop dead?"

Half an hour later, of course, you have worked out a precise statement that is a combination of clever wit and wholesome witness, but by then your friend (and the opportunity) is long gone. Does your attack of "slow witness" and quick temper mean that you can never hope to walk in the Spirit?

Hardly. Realistic Christians are ready for momentary defeats, *but they never go into permanent retreat.* It would take a perfect person to continually walk in the Spirit without one mis-

(v) to dwell in a ... for a time in a ... space ... a temp stay.

step. Perfect people are in short supply this side of eternity.

The thing to do is start each day with a definite decision that, *by faith*, you will walk in the Spirit and not live only to please yourself. When you sin, confess it on the spot if you can remember to do so. *And keep going.* For many Christians walking in the Spirit becomes a self-centered sojourn, because they don't have the backbone to admit to God (and others) that they're wrong and then get their lives back on track and go on from there. If you really want to walk in the Spirit, no one is standing in your way but you. Go ahead and take the first step.

The Holy Spirit does still more for Christians. Through the Spirit Christians have hope. Life is not a dead-end street. Christians look forward to the day when even their bodies will no longer be victim to decay and death. They will have new bodies, bodies that will never die.

ROMANS 8:18-27

[18]Yet what we suffer now is nothing compared to the glory he will give us later. [19]For all creation is waiting eagerly for that future day when God will reveal who his children really are. [20]Against its will, everything on earth was subjected to God's curse. [21]All creation anticipates the day when it will join God's children in glorious freedom from death and decay. [22]For we know that all creation has been groaning as in the pains of childbirth right up to the present time. [23]And even we Christians, although we have the Holy Spirit within us as a foretaste of future glory, also groan to be released from pain and suffering. We, too, wait anxiously for that day when God will give us our full rights as his children, including the new bodies he has promised us. [24]Now that we are saved, we eagerly look forward to this freedom. For if you

already have something, you don't need to hope for it. [25]But if we look forward to something we don't have yet, we must wait patiently and confidently.

[26]And the Holy Spirit helps us in our distress. For we don't even know what we should pray for, nor how we should pray. But the Holy Spirit prays for us with groanings that cannot be expressed in words. [27]And the Father who knows all hearts knows what the Spirit is saying, for the Spirit pleads for us believers in harmony with God's own will.

YOUR PROBLEMS AND HIS PROBLEMS

Christians can face the future unafraid. They have more than a set of religious precepts. They are related to the living God.

God's Holy Spirit is already at work within you. He even prays for you. Your daily problems are no longer yours alone. He is there with you all the time—if only you will give Him complete control.

FOR FURTHER THOUGHT

1. Look at the cartoons on pp. 66 and 67. Does the dilemma that Paul describes in Romans 7:15-21 ring true in your own life? Can you see a particular area of your life where you have a difficult time doing what you want to do or not doing what you don't want to do?

2. Memorize Romans 8:5 from the *New Living Translation*.

3. Compare Romans 8:1-11 with Galatians 5:16-25. Write a brief statement describing the difference between

being a Christian (being controlled by the Spirit, living to please God) and being religious (being controlled by your ego, living to please yourself). Note especially Galatians 5:16-18. Should a Christian have to force himself to obey God's laws? Why?

4. Reread Galatians 5:19-21 and identify any sins mentioned there that are reflected in your own life as the result of living to please yourself. Be honest and specific, not fuzzy and pseudospiritual. Then bring those sins before God and ask for His forgiveness. Make a daily commitment to walk in the Spirit by faith, not by sight or your own strength. When the Holy Spirit controls your life, He can take the impure results of selfish living and turn them into the positive fruit mentioned in Galatians 5:22-23: "Love, joy, peace, patience, kindness, goodness, faithfulness, gentleness, and self-control."

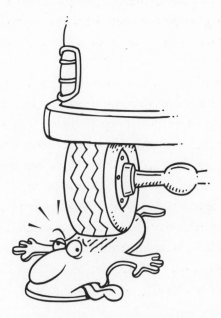

CHAPTER 7

How Can ALL Things Work Together for Good?

Yes, how can they? Christians love to quote this verse—to *other* people who have troubles. But how many of us really believe it? How many have put Romans 8:28 to a test, or more importantly, have been tested by it? How can death, accidents, personal failures and predicaments "work for your good"? Is this just Christian "sour grapes" rationalizing? Before deciding, look more closely at what Paul actually says.

ROMANS 8:28-30

> [28]And we know that God causes everything to work together for the good of those who love God and are called according to his purpose for them. [29]For God knew his people in advance, and he chose them to become like his Son, so that his Son would be the first-born, with many brothers and sisters. [30]And having chosen them, he called them to come to him. And he gave them right standing with himself, and he promised them his glory.

NOT "WHY" BUT "TO WHAT END"?

Does Romans 8:28 make sense for the Christian? Perfect sense. In fact, it makes sense *only* for the Christian. Let's read this verse again: "And we know that God causes everything to work together for the good of *those who love God*" (emphasis added). Here is the all-important condition: "Those who love God."

Loving God is something a Christian certainly wants to do. "We love him, because he first loved us" (1 John 4:19, *NKJV*). Problem is, it's easier to love God when things are going well than when things are going wrong. In fact, that is a good test: Just how much do I love God when the going gets rough? Do I let circumstances get the best of me?

Instead of loving God and trusting Him when things go wrong, I can always resort to self-pity. There is nobody I would

rather feel sorry for than myself. But feeling sorry for myself doesn't get me anywhere.

Is Romans 8:28 trying to tell me that God is *in my circumstances*? He has allowed this thing to happen, this disappointment, this frustration, perhaps even a tragedy. But if I know that God loves me and I love Him, then my question is not "Why?" but "To what end?"

But perhaps I decide not to feel mere self-pity over circumstances. I can always give way to discouragement. Everything is going against me. The ball just isn't bouncing my way. Nobody understands. Nobody cares about what I am trying to do. Nobody wants to help.

Nobody? Romans 8:28 says, "those who love God." First John 4:19 says that we love God because He first loved us. And so here I am—my circumstances, myself and God. Here is where "religion" is not enough. I need a Person. Someone who understands, who cares, who will help me up off the floor to try again. Christ is ready to do this if I am willing to respond to His love with love and trust of my own.

But of course if I really want to go down the tube of circumstances, I can become bitter. You've met people who are bitter. Life has played a dirty trick on them. They just didn't get the breaks. When Christians become bitter against life, against the Church, even against God, they cut themselves off from the resource they need most: knowing that God loves them and will help them.

But there is one more condition to Romans 8:28: "God causes everything to work together for the good of those who are *called according to his purpose for them*" (emphasis added), or as *The Living Bible* puts it: "are fitting into His plans."

And just what are His plans? Go on to verse 29: God's purpose is that we "become like his Son." This doesn't mean we are to become celestial carbon copies. God always gives freedom to choose, to be an individual, a person. But God also knows our weaknesses, our problems, our sins. He sends circumstances into our lives, circumstances that work much as a sculptor works on stone—chipping away that temper or trimming away the pride, the deceit, the jealousy. Each Christian is a different creation, but God works on us all, *for our good*, with His Son as the model.

When you read Romans 8:28 in context, you begin to see how things *do* work together for good. No matter what happens, we know that behind it is God's plan, purpose and, above all, His love. Paul goes on to talk about that love as he brings Romans 8 to a climax. He has left the Death Valley of Romans 7 far behind. He's about to finish scaling a spiritual peak that towers higher than Mount Everest. Through Christ, Paul knows that he is more than a conqueror.

ROMANS 8:31-39

31What can we say about such wonderful things as these? If God is for us, who can ever be against us? 32Since God did not spare even his own Son but gave him up for us all, won't God, who gave us Christ, also give us everything else?

33Who dares accuse us whom God has chosen for his own? Will God? No! He is the one who has given us right standing with himself. 34Who then will condemn us? Will Christ Jesus? No, for he is the one who died for us and was raised to life for us and is sitting at the place of highest honor next to God, pleading for us.

35Can anything ever separate us from Christ's love? Does it mean he no longer loves us if we have trouble or calamity, or are persecuted, or are hungry or cold or in danger or threatened with death? 36(Even the Scriptures say, "For your sake we are killed every day;

we are being slaughtered like sheep.") [37]No, despite all these things, overwhelming victory is ours through Christ, who loved us.

[38]And I am convinced that nothing can ever separate us from his love. Death can't, and life can't. The angels can't, and the demons can't. Our fears for today, our worries about tomorrow, and even the powers of hell can't keep God's love away. [39]Whether we are high above the sky or in the deepest ocean, nothing in all creation will ever be able to separate us from the love of God that is revealed in Christ Jesus our Lord.

The Greatest Power We Know

Can you believe this? *Will* you believe this? If you will, God can change your life. You will be able to live confidently no matter what tests may come your way. No matter what happens, nothing can change God's love for you. That's worth thinking about when danger, trouble, an accident or death strikes. Sometimes Christians feel that they should be delivered from accidents, sickness and death. And when troubles come, they ask: "Why did God let this happen to me?"

The Bible does not promise escape from suffering. If it did, then everybody would become a Christian—just to avoid accidents, troubles, heart attacks, cancer. That might be a good motive for being religious, but it's a poor motive for being a Christian.

Instead, God offers us His presence in all of life's troubles. He tells us that nothing can ever shake His love for us. For the Christian, every cloud doesn't have a silver lining, *but behind the clouds the sun is always shining.*

Prose really can't do these last lines of Romans 8 justice, but perhaps the following poem by Ralph Carmichael begins to catch the substance of Paul's thought.

We Are More Than Conquerors

We are more than conquerors
Through Him that loved us so,
The Christ that dwells within us
Is the Greatest Power we know.
He will fight beside us
Though the enemy is great;
Who can stand against us?
He's the Captain of our fate.
Then we will conquer, never fear,
So let the battle rage;
He has promised to be near,
Until the end of the age.
We are more than conquerors
Through Him that loved us so,
The Christ that dwells within us
Is the Greatest Power we know.[1]

"The Christ who dwells within you" is the key to "sanctification," to having power to live the Christian life. Believe Christ, trust Him, walk with Him in the Spirit, respond to His love with your own. This is the difference between being a Christian and settling for "being religious."

FOR FURTHER THOUGHT

1. Memorize Romans 8:28 from the *New Living Translation*. Focus on the phrase "God causes everything to work together" and list any problems, setbacks or defeats you are now facing. Next, list the victories, accomplishments and progress you are now enjoying.

2. Read Romans 8:28-30 in as many Bible translations as you can. Do you feel "called according to his purpose"? Compare this passage with Ephesians 1:5,11 and 1 Peter 1:2,20. What is God's purpose for you?

3. Compare Romans 8:37-39 with 1 Corinthians 15:54-58. Then write a brief statement that begins with "Overwhelming victory is mine through Jesus Christ because."

CHAPTER 8

Who Can Know the Mind of God?

At this point in his letter to the Romans, Paul inserts what some call a "parenthesis." He stops to talk about "the fly in the ointment" as far as he is concerned: the rejection of God's plan of salvation in Christ by his own kinsmen—the Jews. Paul knows that God is bound to the Jews by solemn covenants. Are these just paper promises? Has God gone back on His word by offering salvation to the Gentiles? Is God capricious? Or is there a flaw in His plan? Read chapters 9—11 carefully. You will see that this parenthesis is, in another sense, a major girder in building a bridge to understanding the vital differences between Christianity, a trusting response to a sovereign God who reaches down to man, and religion, man's reaching up to please or promote a god he has made himself.

ROMANS 9:1-33

¹In the presence of Christ, I speak with utter truthfulness—I do not lie—and my conscience and the Holy Spirit confirm that what I am saying is true. ²My heart is filled with bitter sorrow and unending grief ³for my people, my Jewish brothers and sisters. I would be willing to be forever cursed—cut off from Christ!—if that would save them. ⁴They are the people of Israel, chosen to be God's special children. God revealed his glory to them. He made covenants with them and gave his law to them. They have the privilege of worshiping him and receiving his wonderful promises. ⁵Their ancestors were great people of God, and Christ himself was a Jew as far as his human nature is concerned. And he is God, who rules over everything and is worthy of eternal praise! Amen.

⁶Well then, has God failed to fulfill his promise to the Jews? No, for not everyone born into a Jewish family is truly a Jew! ⁷Just the fact that they are descendants of Abraham doesn't make them truly Abraham's children. For the Scriptures say, "Isaac is the son through whom your descendants will be counted," though Abraham had other children, too. ⁸This means that Abraham's physical descendants are not necessarily children of God. It is the children of the promise who are considered to be

Abraham's children. [9]For God had promised, "Next year I will return, and Sarah will have a son."

[10]This son was our ancestor Isaac. When he grew up, he married Rebekah, who gave birth to twins. [11]But before they were born, before they had done anything good or bad, she received a message from God. (This message proves that God chooses according to his own plan, [12]not according to our good or bad works.) She was told, "The descendants of your older son will serve the descendants of your younger son." [13]In the words of the Scriptures, "I loved Jacob, but I rejected Esau."

[14]What can we say? Was God being unfair? Of course not! [15]For God said to Moses, "I will show mercy to anyone I choose, and I will show compassion to anyone I choose."

[16]So receiving God's promise is not up to us. We can't get it by choosing it or working hard for it. God will show mercy to anyone he chooses.

[17]For the Scriptures say that God told Pharaoh, "I have appointed you for the very purpose of displaying my power in you, and so that my fame might spread throughout the earth." [18]So you see, God shows mercy to some just because he wants to, and he chooses to make some people refuse to listen.

[19]Well then, you might say, "Why does God blame people for not listening? Haven't they simply done what he made them do?"

[20]No, don't say that. Who are you, a mere human being, to criticize God? Should the thing that was created say to the one who made it, "Why have you made me like this?" [21]When a potter makes jars out of clay, doesn't he have a right to use the same lump of clay to make one jar for decoration and another to throw garbage

into? ²²God has every right to exercise his judgment and his power, but he also has the right to be very patient with those who are the objects of his judgment and are fit only for destruction. ²³He also has the right to pour out the riches of his glory upon those he prepared to be the objects of his mercy—²⁴even upon us, whom he selected, both from the Jews and from the Gentiles.

²⁵Concerning the Gentiles, God says in the prophecy of Hosea, "Those who were not my people, I will now call my people. And I will love those whom I did not love before."

²⁶And, "Once they were told, 'You are not my people.' But now he will say, 'You are children of the living God.'"

²⁷Concerning Israel, Isaiah the prophet cried out, "Though the people of Israel are as numerous as the sand on the seashore, only a small number will be saved. ²⁸For the Lord will carry out his sentence upon the earth quickly and with finality."

²⁹And Isaiah said in another place, "If the Lord Almighty had not spared a few of us, we would have been wiped out as completely as Sodom and Gomorrah."

³⁰Well then, what shall we say about these things? Just this: The Gentiles have been made right with God by faith, even though they were not seeking him. ³¹But the Jews, who tried so hard to get right with God by keeping the law, never succeeded. ³²Why not? Because they were trying to get right with God by keeping the law and being good instead of by depending on faith. They stumbled over the great rock in their path. ³³God warned them of this in the Scriptures when he said, "I am placing a stone in Jerusalem that causes people to stumble, and a rock that makes them fall. But anyone who believes in him will not be disappointed."

WHO'S IN CHARGE HERE?

God is not on trial. He runs the world according to His will. He is sovereign. We are His creation. Therefore, we have no business judging our creator. We are not to be critics of God. He is our critic. We are not to put God on trial. He alone is the supreme Judge. Each one of us must stand his or her own trial.

But it is not only because of God's wrath that He turns down an Esau or a Pharaoh and then turns around to have mercy on His chosen people. God knew before Esau was born how he would act and what he would do. On the basis of such careless behavior by Esau, God rejected him. Pharaoh was rejected not because God decided to be mean, but because Pharaoh refused to acknowledge the Lord. Pharaoh hardened his heart against God's miraculous revelation.

The problem is never with a holy God but with sinful man.

Questions will always persist. Our knowledge is limited since we are only created beings and not the Creator. Since God is loving and merciful (and we are confident of this because of Jesus Christ!), the miracle is not that God rejects sinful men but that He is merciful to those who scarcely deserve it. The miracle is that He has not yet destroyed the world.

But what has this to do with the Jews and their rejection of Christ?

ROMANS 10:1-21

Dear brothers and sisters, the longing of my heart and my prayer to God is that the Jewish people might be saved. [2]I know what enthusiasm they have for God, but it is misdirected zeal. [3]For they don't understand God's way of making people right with himself. Instead, they are clinging to their own way of getting right with God by trying to keep the law. They won't go along with God's way. ⁴For Christ has accomplished the whole purpose of the law. All who believe in him are made right with God.

⁵For Moses wrote that the law's way of making a person right with God requires obedience to all of its commands. ⁶But the way of getting right with God through faith says, "You don't need to go to heaven" (to find Christ and bring him down to help you). ⁷And it says, "You don't need to go to the place of the dead" (to bring Christ back to life again). ⁸Salvation that comes from trusting Christ—which is the message we preach—is already within easy reach. In fact, the Scriptures say, "The message is close at hand; it is on your lips and in your heart."

⁹For if you confess with your mouth that Jesus is Lord and believe in your heart that God raised him from the dead, you will be saved. ¹⁰For it is by believing in your heart that you are made right with God, and it is by confessing with your mouth that you are saved. ¹¹As the Scriptures tell us, "Anyone who believes in him will not be disappointed." ¹²Jew and Gentile are the same in this respect. They all have the same Lord, who generously gives his riches to all who ask for them. ¹³For "Anyone who calls on the name of the Lord will be saved."

¹⁴But how can they call on him to save them unless they believe in him? And how can they believe in him if they have never heard about him? And how can they hear about him unless someone tells them? ¹⁵And how will anyone go and tell them without being sent? That is what the Scriptures mean when they say, "How beautiful are the feet of those who bring good news!"

¹⁶But not everyone welcomes the Good News, for Isaiah the prophet said, "Lord, who has believed our message?" ¹⁷Yet faith comes from listening to this message of good news—the Good News about Christ.

¹⁸But what about the Jews? Have they actually heard the message? Yes, they have: "The message of God's creation has gone out to everyone, and its words to all the world."

¹⁹But did the people of Israel really understand? Yes, they did, for even in the time of Moses, God had said, "I will rouse your jealousy by blessing other nations. I will make you angry by blessing the foolish Gentiles."

²⁰And later Isaiah spoke boldly for God: "I was found by people who were not looking for me. I showed myself to those who were not asking for me."

²¹But regarding Israel, God said, "All day long I opened my arms to them, but they kept disobeying me and arguing with me."

LIVING BY THE LAW IS A DEAD-END STREET

Paul makes one thing clear in this passage: Religious zeal is not enough.

The Jews thought they could make themselves right with God through meticulous obedience to the laws and observance of customs. There are many striking examples and anecdotes about the lengths Jews would go to obey the Law.

For example, the second book of Maccabees (part of the Apocrypha) tells about a Jewish scribe named Eleazar. During the siege of Jerusalem by Antiochus Epiphanes, Eleazar was ordered to eat pork that had been sacrificed to Zeus in the Temple.

This was forbidden under Jewish law. In strict adherence to the Law, Eleazar refused. The men in charge of the sacrifice, who had known Eleazar for a long time, urged him to eat some meat that was proper to eat and pretend he was eating the sacrificial pork. Eleazar refused, and he was beaten with whips until he died. As he died he prayed, "I am dying by fiery torments for the Law's sake" (2 Maccabees 6:28). Eleazar resisted to the death *for the Law's sake.* He died for a law that forbade him to eat pork! A rather pointless death, you say? Not to Eleazar, not to the Jew who believed that living by the Law was the way to God.

But Paul informs his kinsmen of the truth that was revealed to him on the Damascus Road: You don't have to reach up to God by trying to keep His laws (see Rom. 10:4-7). You simply respond to God as He reaches down to you. You believe (in your heart, not just your head) that Jesus is Lord and confess (with your mouth) that He is your Savior from sin. And whether you are Jew or Gentile, God accepts you.

One more point . . . Paul reminds the Jews that God's plan never was limited to one nation (see Rom. 10:19-20). The prophets spoke long ago of how God would be found by people *who weren't even looking for Him.*

But where does this leave the Jews? What does it mean to be one of God's chosen nation? Here is Paul's conclusion.

ROMANS 11:1-33

¹I ask, then, has God rejected his people, the Jews? Of course not! Remember that I myself am a Jew, a descendant of Abraham and a member of the tribe of Benjamin.

²No, God has not rejected his own people, whom he chose from the very beginning. Do you remember what the Scriptures say about this? Elijah the prophet

complained to God about the people of Israel and said, [3]"Lord, they have killed your prophets and torn down your altars. I alone am left, and now they are trying to kill me, too."

[4]And do you remember God's reply? He said, "You are not the only one left. I have seven thousand others who have never bowed down to Baal!"

[5]It is the same today, for not all the Jews have turned away from God. A few are being saved as a result of God's kindness in choosing them. [6]And if they are saved by God's kindness, then it is not by their good works. For in that case, God's wonderful kindness would not be what it really is—free and undeserved.

[7]So this is the situation: Most of the Jews have not found the favor of God they are looking for so earnestly. A few have—the ones God has chosen—but the rest were made unresponsive. [8]As the Scriptures say, "God has put them into a deep sleep. To this very day he has shut their eyes so they do not see, and closed their ears so they do not hear."

[9]David spoke of this same thing when he said, "Let their bountiful table become a snare, a trap that makes them think all is well. Let their blessings cause them to stumble. [10]Let their eyes go blind so they cannot see, and let their backs grow weaker and weaker."

[11]Did God's people stumble and fall beyond recovery? Of course not! His purpose was to make his salvation available to the Gentiles, and then the Jews would be jealous and want it for themselves. [12]Now if the Gentiles were enriched because the Jews turned down God's offer of salvation, think how much greater a blessing the world will share when the Jews finally accept it.

[13]I am saying all of this especially for you Gentiles. God has appointed me as the apostle to the Gentiles. I lay great

stress on this, [14]for I want to find a way to make the Jews want what you Gentiles have, and in that way I might save some of them. [15]For since the Jews' rejection meant that God offered salvation to the rest of the world, how much more wonderful their acceptance will be. It will be life for those who were dead! [16]And since Abraham and the other patriarchs were holy, their children will also be holy. For if the roots of the tree are holy, the branches will be, too.

[17]But some of these branches from Abraham's tree, some of the Jews, have been broken off. And you Gentiles, who were branches from a wild olive tree, were grafted in. So now you also receive the blessing God has promised Abraham and his children, sharing in God's rich nourishment of his special olive tree. [18]But you must be careful not to brag about being grafted in to replace the branches that were broken off. Remember, you are just a branch, not the root.

[19]"Well," you may say, "those branches were broken off to make room for me." [20]Yes, but remember—those branches, the Jews, were broken off because they didn't believe God, and you are there because you do believe. Don't think highly of yourself, but fear what could happen. [21]For if God did not spare the branches he put there in the first place, he won't spare you either.

[22]Notice how God is both kind and severe. He is severe to those who disobeyed, but kind to you as you continue to trust in his kindness. But if you stop trusting, you also will be cut off. [23]And if the Jews turn from their unbelief, God will graft them back into the tree again. He has the power to do it.

[24]For if God was willing to take you who were, by nature, branches from a wild olive tree and graft you into his own good tree—a very unusual thing to do—he will be

far more eager to graft the Jews back into the tree where they belong.

[25]I want you to understand this mystery, dear brothers and sisters, so that you will not feel proud and start bragging. Some of the Jews have hard hearts, but this will last only until the complete number of Gentiles comes to Christ. [26]And so all Israel will be saved. Do you remember what the prophets said about this? "A Deliverer will come from Jerusalem, and he will turn Israel from all ungodliness. [27]And then I will keep my covenant with them and take away their sins."

[28]Many of the Jews are now enemies of the Good News. But this has been to your benefit, for God has given his gifts to you Gentiles. Yet the Jews are still his chosen people because of his promises to Abraham, Isaac, and Jacob. [29]For God's gifts and his call can never be withdrawn. [30]Once, you Gentiles were rebels against God, but when the Jews refused his mercy, God was merciful to you instead. [31]And now, in the same way, the Jews are the rebels, and God's mercy has come to you. But someday they, too, will share in God's mercy. [32]For God has imprisoned all people in their own disobedience so he could have mercy on everyone.

[33]Oh, what a wonderful God we have! How great are his riches and wisdom and knowledge! How impossible it is for us to understand his decisions and his methods!

THERE'S NO SALVATION IN THE "ESTABLISHMENT"

In the first verses of chapter 11 of his letter to the Romans, Paul repeats what he said in chapter 9. God does not save nations;

He saves individuals. The correct question is not "Has God discarded His people, the Jews?" The correct question is "Which Jews are responding to God's gift of salvation in Christ?" It was precisely on this point that the Jews made a fatal error. They forgot that from the start God's terms were personal responsibility and individual faith. The Jews started thinking that they had salvation because of being members of a special nation. They became, in a way, "organization men." They used the Law to promote their own version of the "Establishment."

And so God cut many of them off, "broke them off," if you want to use Paul's illustration of the olive tree (Rom. 11:17). And Paul warns the Gentiles to not start feeling smug. They are grafted into the olive tree for one reason: their faith. This is God's plan right now, but He has not forgotten His covenant with the Jews. Even though most of them are now enemies of the gospel, there will come a day when they will be saved through God's mercy.

Hard to grasp? Yes, it is. It is enough to convince you that no one can know or completely understand the mind of God.

ROMANS 11:34-36

34For who can know what the Lord is thinking? Who knows enough to be his counselor? 35And who could ever give him so much that he would have to pay it back? 36For everything comes from him; everything exists by his power and is intended for his glory. To him be glory evermore. Amen.

COULD YOU TRUST A GOD WHO WASN'T IN CHARGE?

If God does not rule, then all our other beliefs about God matter very little. If God is not sovereign, we cannot trust Him.

How can you trust a God who is not in charge?

The Lord is King. He is to be worshiped, not used. He is to be adored, not merely made attractive. His wisdom is beyond us. He makes His own decisions without asking for our poor opinions.

We can do little else but acknowledge that God is God. At the end of this probing section in which Paul has tried to find out answers to some real questions, he can only fall on his knees in wonder and praise of God. He is overwhelmed at the wisdom which lies beyond him. He can only worship. God, in Christ, is a person, not a religion.

There is a famous statue of Christ in Brazil. But the face of Jesus is so turned that the only way to look into His eyes is to get down on your knees and look up.

That is the only way to see God, too—in humility and faith. This is how to be a Christian without being religious.

FOR FURTHER THOUGHT

1. God's sovereignty and man's freedom are a seeming paradox that is often hard to understand. If God were not sovereign, what kind of God would He be? And if man were not free to either choose or reject God, what would man be? Discuss your thoughts with someone, and then write out a paragraph summing up your answers to these two questions.
2. Compare Romans 11:33-36 with Romans 8:28-39. Make a list of ways these two passages tie together.

CHAPTER 9

Is It God's Will?

All Christians ask this question. Some ask sincerely, with real concern. Some are curious. Some are worried, even afraid. Some ask too late, after they have gone ahead with ill-fated plans. Some try "formulas" like "Read a chapter a day and pray." Others see God's will as a sort of career computer—a "master plan" that guarantees you the right job. Whatever the motive, whatever the means for finding an answer, the question of God's will dogs the Christian's steps with "unhurrying chase and unperturbed pace."[1] But instead of playing religious roulette with formulas and master plans, perhaps we should first ask if being in God's will is a Christian's destination or a way of traveling. Paul knew the road well.

ROMANS 12:1-2

[1]And so, dear brothers and sisters, I plead with you to give your bodies to God. Let them be a living and holy sacrifice—the kind he will accept. When you think of what he has done for you, is this too much to ask? [2]Don't copy the behavior and customs of this world, but let God transform you into a new person by changing the way you think. Then you will know what God wants you to do, and you will know how good and pleasing and perfect his will really is.

DO YOU HAVE YOUR CART AHEAD OF YOUR HORSE?

Romans 12:1 . . . used frequently in memory verse lists and often the text for the speaker's closing challenge at a Christian camp or conference . . . but also the hinge on which the book of Romans turns to take a new tack.

For 11 chapters Paul has dealt with what a Christian believes and why. He has told you how to know Christ and be saved from the penalty of sin. He has told you how to be empowered by Christ and be freed from the power of sin. Now, with the start of chapter 12, he begins telling you how to serve Christ—in effect, how to find and do God's will.

Alan Redpath has described God's will as twofold. The will of God concerning character is *universal*, but the will of God concerning service is *individual*.[2] All right, you'll probably buy that. It's easy to see that God wants you to develop in Christian character. But the service angle—just what you should do and when and how to do it—this is the stickler; so what good does it do to know that God's will has two parts?

Just this. A lot of Christians put the cart before the horse. They fume and fret about what God wants them to do (service) when they are spiritually unprepared to do it (character). Here is where Romans 12:1 comes in. Before God wants your service, He wants a guarantee that He really has *you*. Paul doesn't mince words. We are to give our bodies as a living sacrifice.

STEP ONE IN FINDING GOD'S WILL: PRESENT YOUR BODY AS A LIVING SACRIFICE.

Sounds almost primitive, doesn't it? How personal can Paul get? It's not too hard to sit in church and promise God your soul and your spirit. After all, it is proper for God to have these things—they are His responsibility with heaven and all that coming up some day. But our *bodies*? Really, this relationship may be getting a bit too close for comfort. This could cramp one's style, get in the way, cause inhibitions. Why, this sort of thing could lead to being more than religious!

Exactly.

God didn't just save your soul. He saved *you*—your total self—and this includes your body. When a Christian gets serious enough about Christ to commit his body—what he does with hands, eyes, ears, mouth—to God, then he is ready to know and do God's will.

Too much to ask? Perhaps, but before you protest, think, says Paul, of what Christ did for you.

As you remember that Christ died for your sins—allowing His body to be broken for you—it's easier to see why the first step in the process is God's will for your character. You cannot fulfill

God's purpose for your character until you present your body—
your total you—to God in an intelligent, determined act of ded-
ication and commitment. You don't do this once a year at camp
or during the annual evangelistic crusade. You do it daily. And as
you give all of yourself to God, you put the horse where it
belongs—in front of the cart. You are ready to move and act within God's will. The power you need (your Christian character)
is where it can do some good (in Christian service).

All right, let's say you do all this. In which direction do you
head? What about service, specifically *specific* service?

A good test of a lot of your plans and activities is right in
Romans 12:2: "Don't copy the behavior and customs of this
world" or as *The New Testament in Modern English* puts it: "Don't
let the world around you squeeze you into its own mould."

This is not to say that you're supposed to become some kind
of oddball. But you are to steer clear of the world's superficial
value system, which places a premium on sensuality, sex and sick
humor. The Christian often faces some tough decisions regarding what is "worldly" and what is acceptable to God. A key
checkpoint is your motive. As J. P. Morgan once said: "A man
always has two reasons for doing anything—a 'good' reason and
the real reason." The particular situation may be difficult but
the choice is usually clear: Are you trying to please yourself, the
"in group," the crowd? Or are you interested in pleasing God?

"All very good," you say, "but the world is very real, and I am
in it all day long. How do I resist the squeeze, stay out of the
mold?" Romans 12:2 goes on to suggest: "Let God transform
you into a new person by changing the way you think."

Surveys and polls show that many Christians are being
sucked into the postmodern mind-set: *All truth is relative and there
are no absolutes.* Morals are up for grabs. Like the proverbial frog
in the kettle, many Christians are being cooked by a secular culture that bombards them daily with messages designed to make

them more concerned with "personal freedom of choice" and "what feels right" rather than "Is it right or is it wrong?" or, more importantly, *"Is it God's will for me?"*

It would be interesting to know how many Christians outwardly claim to be interested in knowing God's will yet are hooked in one way or another by the continuous bombardment, in ads,

WELL, WHEN YOU PUT IT THAT WAY...

DOES GOD ASK FOR TOO MUCH? REMEMBER WHAT HE DID FOR YOU.

TV and magazines, that is designed to increase the appetite for sex, things, pleasure. Not that there is anything wrong with sex, things and pleasure. It's just that few of us really need stimulation of our appetites in these areas. There is plenty of appetite there already, and it's a case of learning how to control these natural drives and desires and bring them into line with the subject of this chapter—God's will.

But even policing your TV programs and censoring your subscriptions isn't the final answer. And Paul knew it, because he advises in Romans 12:2 to become a "new person by changing the way you think."

The trap that snares a lot of Christians is the old dual standard: one set of rules for outward behavior and another standard for the mind—the "thought life." It's not hard to learn how to play the game called "churchianity." You learn to not do certain things—or at least not to get caught doing them. You learn to show up at church often enough to be labeled "active" or "faithful." You look pretty spiritual, and all the while your thought life is running "amuck in muck" or feasting on materialism, greed, hatred, jealousy, etc.

So what do you do? If you want God's will, give Him your total self—a living sacrifice—and that means your body *and* your mind, which He can renew from within, if you let Him.

Perhaps by now you are getting the message: God's will is not something you order by mail. You don't use formulas, but there are checkpoints to apply to any situation. F. B. Meyer, a famous preacher of his day, was on a sea voyage. Coming into port one night, it was very stormy and the entrance to the harbor looked very narrow. Meyer turned to the captain on the bridge beside him and said, "Captain, how do you know when to make the turn into the harbor?"

"That's an art," said the captain. "Do you see those three lights on shore? When they're all in a straight line, I go right in."

Alan Redpath applies this story to finding God's will by pointing out three "navigation lights" that are available to the Christian for guidance: The Bible, the inward witness of the Holy Spirit and outward circumstances.[3] When these three are in line, go on in. Until they are, try to wait. Waiting is hard, but often it can be the best thing to do.

Let's look at these three lights more closely.

The Bible

The guidance of God's Word is primary. It's interesting to note that many of us say we are interested in God's will, but we balk at checking our plans and habits against the plain teaching of the Bible. How can you say you are seeking God's will, if you don't know what the Bible says? This is like going to someone for advice but not letting him or her talk. You actually want that person to agree with everything you say.

Another mistaken concept is to treat the Bible like an "answer book." You page through, trying to find "just the right verse" to help you out. The Bible is God's message, His conversation with you. If you are serious about communicating with God, start talking to Him—and let Him talk to you. This is the first step in walking in the Spirit. (See chapter 6 for a review of walking in the Spirit.)

The Inward Witness of the Holy Spirit

The witness of the Holy Spirit comes as you walk in the Spirit. Prayer is vital here. It's unfortunate that we have made "I'll have to pray about it" something of a cliché. Maybe we should change the phrase to "I will talk with God about it." Remember, prayer is talking with God, not at God. Some prayer lists sound like Christmas lists. Others sound like assignments that God should carry out because we are "so spiritual, so deserving."

The inner witness of the Spirit is always available. It comes from walking and living in the Spirit, but this is a constant, daily reality, not some button you push when you think you "need a little advice" from God.

Outward Circumstances

Take a look at outward circumstances last. We usually reverse the order. *First,* we call a committee meeting. *First,* we examine all the evidence. *First,* we talk it over with so-and-so or read up on the subject. But if you start with circumstances, you seldom get beyond them. How can you evaluate circumstances if you have no guidance from God's Word and God's Spirit?

But suppose you feel you have the Word and the Spirit lined up fairly well. How do you evaluate or act upon circumstances? This process can be intriguing and exciting. For one thing you have to act in faith on what you already know. Is it evident that there are certain actions that would be worth taking? Some people call this "trying different doors." Sometimes God will slam shut every door except the one He wants you to walk through. You may have to try several doors to learn which is the right one.

No, God's will doesn't drop out of the blue in a special delivery letter. But He has written to you—in His Word. He will talk to you through the inner witness of His Spirit. And He will guide you as you weigh outward circumstances.

Still sound like a formula? Well, you can make it that. You can be "very religious" about these three checkpoints—or you can use them like a Christian, in faith, trust and commitment. Then you will see from your own experience how God's ways will really satisfy you.

For other practical pointers on finding God's will, read on in Romans 12 for some tips on how to take an honest look at yourself. Be sure, says Paul, that you see the plus as well as the minus side.

ROMANS 12:3-8

[3]As God's messenger, I give each of you this warning: Be honest in your estimate of yourselves, measuring your value by how much faith God has given you. [4]Just as our bodies have many parts and each part has a special function, [5]so it is with Christ's body. We are all parts of his one body, and each of us has different work to do. And since we are all one body in Christ, we belong to each other, and each of us needs all the others.

[6]God has given each of us the ability to do certain things well. So if God has given you the ability to prophesy, speak out when you have faith that God is speaking through you. [7]If your gift is that of serving others, serve them well. If you are a teacher, do a good job of teaching. [8]If your gift is to encourage others, do it! If you have money, share it generously. If God has given you leadership ability, take the responsibility seriously. And if you have a gift for showing kindness to others, do it gladly.

ONLY ONE THING THAT REALLY COUNTS

Be honest in your estimate, says Paul. Some Christians have a tendency to think they are "no good," always failing, never really accomplishing anything. If you're in this boat, abandon ship right now. God has accepted you. You are a person of worth. Christ died for you. You have potential. Don't sell yourself— or the Lord Jesus Christ—short.

The other side of the honesty coin is for those with the superiority complex. None of us is humanity's gift to God. In fact, God had to send *us* a gift so we could get out of the human snake pit called sin.

As usual, Paul zeroes in on the needful thing: faith. Your *faith* is what matters, not your GPA, SAT score or the number of horses under your hood. Your *faith* is what counts, not the fact that you were once voted "Miss Personality" or "Most Likely to Succeed."

All Christians need each other and we all need Christ. There is work to do—serving, teaching, preaching, making (and *giving*) money, just plain being kind to others and much more. And, as you will see in the next chapter, Paul has some explicit words on how to get on with it.

FOR FURTHER THOUGHT

1. Study Romans 12:1 in as many translations as you can and choose one to memorize. Compare it with Matthew 16:24 and Luke 9:23. What does "self-denial" mean to you? What does self-denial have to do with Romans 12:1?

2. Romans 12:2 from *The New Testament in Modern English* says, "Don't let the world around you squeeze you into its own mould, but let God re-make you so that your whole attitude of mind is changed. Thus you will prove in practice that the will of God is good, acceptable to him and perfect." Compare this with the following verses on resisting worldliness: 1 Corinthians 7:31; Galatians 6:14; 2 Timothy 2:4; Hebrews 11:24-26; 1 John 2:15-17. Write a definition of "worldliness," and then list three practical ways to avoid being worldly.

3. Think about the way you seek God's will. Is the cart (your service to God) before your horse (your Christian character)? What aspects of your character do you feel that God wants to refine so that you are ready for the ministry He has for you? Bring these things before God in prayer and commit yourself to Him in faith that He will work in you Christlike character.

4. Think about the three guidelines mentioned in this chapter for finding God's will: the Bible, the inward witness of the Holy Spirit and outward circumstances. Do you make choices based on circumstances or based on seeking God through His Word and Spirit? How can you reorder your priorities so that His guidance and leading come first? Share your ideas with a friend.

5. What are the primary media influences in your life? Do you need to filter out any of these influences? Make a list of the ways, both positive and negative, that you are renewing your mind from within.

CHAPTER 10

Is Your Christianity Actually Counterfeit Love?

Counterfeit love for Christ? Counterfeit Christianity? Not mine! I'll have you know that I'm born again, washed in the blood of the lamb. None of this Mickey Mouse liberalism for me. I *know* I'm on my way to heaven. I've got my doctrine straight, and that's for sure. I serve the Lord, and I even tithe (sometimes). I give my old clothes to missions. I put Scripture references in all my Christmas cards. I, I . . .

But one thing more is needed.

ROMANS 12:9-21

[handwritten: that which wrestle corrupt others]

[handwritten: Gifting have 2 be partnered c̄ love in the body]

[handwritten left margin: bk God hates evil]

9Don't just pretend that you love others. Really love them. Hate what is wrong. Stand on the side of the good. *[handwritten: even when the battle is inside of you]* 10Love each other with genuine affection, and take delight in honoring each other. 11Never be lazy in your work, but serve the Lord enthusiastically.

[handwritten left margin: valuing others based on how God sees you]

12Be glad for all God is planning for you. Be patient in trouble, and always be prayerful. 13When God's children are in need, be the one to help them out. And get into the habit of inviting guests home for dinner or, if they need lodging, for the night.

[handwritten right margin: Receiving the word lesson in the mountain, stay connect & focus]

[handwritten left margin: seek opportunity Don't wait til people ask]

14If people persecute you because you are a Christian, don't curse them; pray that God will bless them. 15When others are happy, be happy with them. If they are sad, share their sorrow. 16Live in harmony with each other. Don't try to act important, but enjoy the company of ordinary people. And don't think you know it all!

17Never pay back evil for evil to anyone. Do things in such a way that everyone can see you are honorable. 18Do your part to live in peace with everyone, as much as possible.

19Dear friends, never avenge yourselves. Leave that to God. For it is written, "I will take vengeance; I will repay those who deserve it," says the Lord.

20Instead, do what the Scriptures say: "If your enemies are hungry, feed them. If they are thirsty, give them something to drink, and they will be ashamed of what they have done to you."

21Don't let evil get the best of you, but conquer evil by doing good.

LET'S QUIT PLAYING "LET'S PRETEND"

Conquer evil by doing good. Paul spent a lot of time at the beginning of his letter to the Romans on the need for believing what is good. Now he is getting down to where we live. In fact, he is starting to sound like a meddler. He wants us to *do* what is good.

Christians speak much of loving God, loving one another, loving mankind. What does all this "lovely" talk mean? For one thing, says Paul, it means that you quit playing "let's pretend." Quit being a phony.

For example, Paul says we should "Hate what is wrong. Stand on the side of the good" (Rom. 12:9). This means more than just staying out of trouble. It means getting involved with trying to change things for the better—where you work, around your school and, above all, in your own home with your own family.

One of the major traps for Christians today is that they are surrounded by so much evil and sin that they grow used to it. They are no longer shocked. They learn to "get along," to keep their mouths shut, to not make trouble. A lot of Christians avoid evil, but *they do not hate it.* A lot of Christians support the good, but *they do not fight for it.* A lot of what is called Christianity is really passive compromise with sin.

But where do you get the power and the motivation to conquer evil by doing good? Love. Genuine love is the needed thing. "Don't just pretend that you love others. Really love them" (v. 9). Romans 12 is a short course in being concerned for others rather than ourselves. This is the hardest thing we can be asked to do. Our psychological makeup demands that we worry first about old Number One. Self-preservation is as natural as breathing. We are quick to defend ourselves and our rights. Our egos are labeled "handle with care." We bruise easily.

And then we become Christians. Suddenly we have no rights, only duties. How unfair can things get? Yes, it would be unfair if the Christian had no resources, no help. To live as Paul suggests in Romans 12 is humanly impossible. It is, however, *supernaturally* possible, as he clearly pointed out back in chapters 6, 7 and 8 of Romans. Walking in the Spirit is not some quaint religious exercise. It is for the street where *you* live.

Paul is getting painfully practical now. You say you are crucified with Christ? You say you have "died to sin and risen again with Christ"? What better way, then, to test all your new powers than to see if you actually can live and love unselfishly. To try to love others unselfishly and at the same time be concerned with standing up for your rights is a contradiction in terms. You cannot serve God and self. You cannot go around with the Bible in one hand while waving your personal Bill of Rights in the other.

"But so few Christians around my church really show unselfish love. Why should I be the one to start the trend?"

Yes, why should you? You probably wouldn't do a very good job of it anyway. People would just think you had suddenly gone a little hyperspiritual or something. You could even lose some social prestige.

There are all kinds of excuses "to not get carried away" with the list of good deeds in Romans 12. But the excuses don't make the standard any less valid. Paul is not nailing up a list of laws that the Christian has to obey without fail. He is setting up goals to aim at, to set your sights on.

Of course you won't do a perfect job of unselfish loving. Of course you may be criticized, even laughed at. But when Paul talks in Romans 12 of honoring others, of never being lax in Christian zeal, of being glad and patient in trouble, of helping others in need and of praying for those who harm you, he is simply putting muscle on the idea of presenting your body as a "living sacrifice" (Rom. 12:1).

This business of being a living sacrifice was well put by a missionary who had this advice for a young fellow who was thinking about the mission field:

Instead of going to the refrigerator for a bite before going to bed or to the corner drugstore for a soda, try going to bed without it. You won't die and you won't miss it when you can't get it out here.

Try cutting the chatter in order to get home earlier or to give more time to studies or devotions. Out here you may have to go for months at a time without friendly chin-fests with others of your own language. Discipline yourself to eat things you don't like, without choking and without griping.

Kick yourself out of bed before the heat comes on in order to spend time with the Lord. Next time you go to camp, try sleeping for two weeks on the floor. Find out if your call and Christian joy vary in inverse proportion to the comforts and conveniences you experience.

I'm not dreaming these things up. I'm thinking of people who so missed ice cream and candy, who couldn't get along without the fellowship of others, who were always complaining of the cold or who couldn't settle down to serious work unless they had eight hours on an innerspring mattress, that they made excuses for not getting the work done. In some cases these were definitely contributing factors to their leaving the field, quitting.

"But I'm not going to the mission field," you say.

Aren't you? Where do you think you are right now? Is your home, school or place of work really any less a mission field than the streets of Bombay or the Auca country of Peru?

Every Christian is a missionary, because a missionary is one who is sent to bring and *to be* the good news to others. Every Christian is called to present his or her body as a living sacrifice. Don't just pretend to love others. Really love them—by going out of your way to help them, by taking their guff, by overlooking their faults, by refusing to retaliate, especially in the sophisticated game of repartee and cutting conversation that so many of us play so well.

Does your Christianity reveal a bogus brand of counterfeit love? Genuine Christian love means first that you sincerely and unselfishly offer your daily life to God. He then proves, tests and tempers your sincerity and unselfishness by sending you out to live with other people, many of whom aren't that lovable.

We all fail, some of us many times, to show perfect Christian love. But faith begins where failure leaves off. We are not only saved from the penalty of sin by faith. We not only conquer sin and temptation by faith. *We also serve and love by faith.*

It is in this living, loving and serving; it is in the daily routine, the "rat race" of life, that you have countless opportunities to be a living sacrifice—or just a burnt offering.

FOR FURTHER THOUGHT

1. Memorize Romans 12:9. Compare this verse with Romans 12:1-2. What is the necessary foundation for genuine Christian love?
2. Some non-Christians seem to show more love than a lot of Christians do. Why is this so?
3. It is easy to complain that it is impossible to love certain obnoxious and irritating individuals—people we just don't like or get along with. Reread Romans 12:9-21 carefully. How many of Paul's suggestions for

loving others depend on how well we like them? What is the difference between liking someone and showing him or her love through your actions?

4. Spend a few minutes praying over your mission field—where you live and work. Ask God to give you opportunities to prove yourself by showing His love to people within your realm of contact and influence.

CHAPTER 11

The Only Law
You Need

"Only one law to obey? Now that wouldn't be so bad. If there's anything that I'm fed up with, it's rules. Regulations. Codes. Curfews. Red tape. Please fill out this form. Please sign your name on all three copies. Traffic laws, tax laws, draft laws. I'm being strangled by authoritarian bureaucracy. One of these days I'll show them. I'm fed up with their overbearing bungling. It's certainly true that the government that governs least governs best. The 'leaster' the better for my money . . ."

Hold on, friend. So you are fed up with this idea of authority, especially the unfairness, the corruption and the unconcerned inefficiency. You want to hear the hammer of justice and the bell of freedom. But first take a look at that "only law you need." Paul's views on authorities and governments may surprise you.

ROMANS 13:1-10

¹Obey the government, for God is the one who put it there. All governments have been placed in power by God. ²So those who refuse to obey the laws of the land are refusing to obey God, and punishment will follow. ³For the authorities do not frighten people who are doing right, but they frighten those who do wrong. So do what they say, and you will get along well. ⁴The authorities are sent by God to help you. But if you are doing something wrong, of course you should be afraid, for you will be punished. The authorities are established by God for that very purpose, to punish those who do wrong. ⁵So you must obey the government for two reasons: to keep from being punished and to keep a clear conscience.

⁶Pay your taxes, too, for these same reasons. For government workers need to be paid so they can keep on doing the work God intended them to do. ⁷Give to everyone what you owe them: Pay your taxes and import duties, and give respect and honor to all to whom it is due.

⁸Pay all your debts, except the debt of love for others. You can never finish paying that! If you love your neighbor, you will fulfill all the requirements of God's law. ⁹For the commandments against adultery and murder and stealing and coveting—and any other commandment—are all summed up in this one commandment:

"Love your neighbor as yourself." [10]Love does no wrong to anyone, so love satisfies all of God's requirements.

ARE YOU BEHIND IN YOUR DEBTS?

Love is the only law you need. Here we are back to love again. But what a strange combination—government and love. What does love have to do with paying taxes or staying within the speed limit?

Everything.

Paul doesn't share these thoughts on obeying civil government because he simply wants to fill space.

In chapter 12, Paul talks about living the Christian life in the daily routine, sharing Christ's love in the daily contact we have with others. It was only natural then that Paul would expand his thinking past the "one-on-one" situations of Romans 12 and comment on living the Christian life as a member of a community, as a citizen of a government.

Wherever there are men, there is government of some kind. And Paul makes one thing crystal clear right at the start: *All governments are in power because God has allowed them to be* (see v. 1).

This means that all governments—even cruel, despotic dictatorships—are part of God's plan and permissive will. Tyrants carry out His purposes along with saints.

When Paul wrote his letter to the church at Rome, the terrible persecutions and martyrdoms of Christians were still a few years away. They would come soon enough in A.D. 64 when Nero needed a scapegoat to explain a terrible fire that leveled most of Rome. Christians were prime suspects for any kind of crime because of their disobedience of Roman law, which demanded that citizens have "no god above Caesar." But Christians *did* have a God above Caesar—the Lord Jesus Christ. They refused to offer sacrifices before statues of the emperor. They worshiped none of the pagan deities or idols which were seen everywhere in Rome. Ironically, their strange beliefs won for Christians the title of "atheist" because, as far as the typical, solid Roman citizen was concerned, they did not believe in the gods.

Although a Jew, Paul was born a Roman citizen. He knew Roman law and the tensions involved for a Christian believer who lived under Roman rule. And so Paul had reasons for including a few words on the Christian concept of citizenship.

For one thing, *Paul did not want Christians to be labeled as being rebellious, as the Jews were.* Palestine was probably Rome's biggest headache. No Jew was content under Roman rule. There was even a band of fanatical Jewish "guerrilla fighters" called Zealots who were pledged to carry on constant terrorism. They would not only cut Roman throats when they could, but they would also burn the crops and homes of fellow Jews who paid tribute to the Roman government. Paul wanted no part of this kind of Jewish insurrection. It would be a direct contradiction of Christian faith and ethics. How could a Christian witness his love for Christ and love for others while cutting someone's throat?

Paul had still more reasons for his teachings on obeying the civil powers. And they apply just as readily today as they did then. For example, *Paul knew that no man can completely disassociate himself from his community.* Being a member of a society brings responsibilities as well as privileges. A man has duties to his nation as well as to his church, even if he does not agree with everything the government stands for or does. Controversy over governments—what kind, how much, how little—has raged since time began. But there is little doubt about the necessity of government. Without the organization and protection of the state, we would all be forced to live by the law of the jungle—survival of the strong and the vicious.

*In addition, the state provides services and advantages that men
could not possibly enjoy individually:* water supply, sewage system,
the courts, schools. No one is free to take everything he or she
can from the state and not give back cooperation and loyalty.

But perhaps Paul's most important reason for advising support of the Roman government was because *he saw Rome as God's
tool for keeping the lid on an otherwise hopelessly explosive situation.*

Paul believed in using the "Pax Romana" (the Roman peace
that prevailed during his time) to the advantage of the gospel.
As long as there was peace, even a rigidly (sometimes cruelly)
enforced one, Paul saw greater opportunity to spread the gospel.
Whether Rome knew it or not, in Paul's mind Rome was helping
him do his missionary work. And for this reason, the wise
Christian would always try to help, not hinder, the state.[1]

And so Paul gives a brief refresher course on good citizenship:
Obey the laws of the land, and respect and cooperate with the
police (if you're innocent, why worry?). Obey the law to keep from
being punished and also because you know it's the right thing to
do. Pay your taxes and fees; obey those in authority; and give
honor and respect to those in high offices (see Rom. 13:1-7).

In verse 8 notice how Paul makes one of his typically fluid
shifts into theological overdrive: "Pay all your debts, except the
debt of love for others. You can never finish paying that!" What
an odd jump in thought, from prosaic things like policemen, taxes
and honoring authorities to the "debt of love." What does Paul
mean?

Simply this: Pay your debts—the money you owe the grocer, the
department store, the used-car lot. Go along with authority wherever you find it: in the corridors of the school, on the streets of the
city, in the aisles and hallways at work. Oil the wheels of social justice. Keep society running as smoothly as possible. Don't offend or
violate the rights of others. *But if you really want motivation and power
to be a good citizen, never stop paying your debt of love to all men.*

And what is this debt of love? To love your neighbor as yourself. Keep this command, this law, and you automatically keep all the others. If you are really concerned with keeping the law of love, it is the only law you really need. Then civil laws are not problems or objects of protests and demonstrations. Civil laws are only guidelines to help you achieve your aim: loving others as you love yourself and thereby fulfilling all of God's requirements.

Most laws, whether biblical, civil or even those laid down in a family, are groups of "thou shalt nots." Laws and rules—at home, at school, at work, in countries—are laid down to prevent the rights of others from being trampled. Laws and rules are necessary to run a society composed of men and women who are under the universal curse of sin. Love is the only law we need, but few of us try or even want to obey it.

What Paul is saying in Romans 13 is that Christians have a distinct responsibility as well as a definite advantage in the area of good citizenship. The Christian citizen's first questions are not "What are my rights? Am I getting justice?" His or her first concern is "Am I living by the law of love?"

By concerning yourself with the positive "dos" of love, you automatically avoid entanglement with a long list of "don'ts" that are necessary to ensure justice for all. Obeying the law of love puts good citizenship in a completely different light. You obey institutional rules and regulations not because you primarily want to avoid trouble but because you seek the common good of all. You obey traffic laws not to stay out of jail or traffic court but because you respect the lives and property of others. You pay your taxes and fees not because you fear a possible chat with IRS but because you believe in government and financing its operation.

Applications of the law of love are endless. Christians who obey the law of love do not cheat or steal. They do not kill or cripple enemies; rather, they try to turn them into friends.

Christians who live by the law of love do not see authority as a threat. Nor do they see imperfections or even gross errors in government as reason to riot or demonstrate unlawfully. Christians are not bystanders in society. Actually they should be in the thick of the battle for justice, morality and changing the system with their vote, not violence. But Christians operate with a different motive. They seek justice for all, yes, but not by simply avoiding or preventing the doing of wrongs to others. The law of love goes beyond justice. The law of love seeks the positive doing of good to others. It is the only law Christians need.

There are still other reasons for good citizenship. Paul closes chapter 13 with a note of realistic urgency, and the crisp language of *The New Living Translation* of the Bible needs no comment, except to suggest that if you are looking for encouragement to live for God, which isn't always the popular thing to do, you might consider this passage.

ROMANS 13:11-14

[11]Another reason for right living is that you know how late it is; time is running out. Wake up, for the coming of our salvation is nearer now than when we first believed. [12]The night is almost gone; the day of salvation will soon be here. So don't live in darkness. Get rid of your evil deeds. Shed them like dirty clothes. Clothe yourselves with the armor of right living, as those who live in the light. [13]We should be decent and true in everything we do, so that everyone can approve of our behavior. Don't participate in wild parties and getting drunk, or in adultery and immoral living, or in fighting and jealousy. [14]But let the Lord Jesus Christ take control of you, and don't think of ways to indulge your evil desires.

For Further Thought

1. Compare Romans 13:1-2 with Ezra 7:26; Ecclesiastes 8:2; Matthew 17:25-27; 22:15-21; Titus 3:1; 1 Peter 2:13-14. Why is government to be obeyed? Could people live together without some form of government? Why?

2. Read Romans 13:1-7 in as many Bible versions as possible. How would you respond to someone who suggests that in this passage Paul is saying that people living under injustice should just accept it as their lot?

3. Compare Romans 13:1-7 with Deuteronomy 16:20; Psalm 82:1-5; Proverbs 21:3; 29:27; Acts 5:17-42 (note v. 29). Do you think that Christians who have fled countries with oppressive governments did the right thing? What if you lived in such a nation and had the chance to get out? What would you do and why?

4. Memorize Romans 13:10. To whom in your family, workplace, school or community do you owe "back payments" on this debt of love? Write down some specific plans for bringing that debt up-to-date.

The Game Christians Play Too Well

"He's okay, but . . ." "Well, I suppose the new plans make some sense, but . . ." "I know I shouldn't judge, but any girl who would . . ." "I suppose I shouldn't say anything; however, I feel it my duty to report that . . ." "Well, they're certainly entitled to their opinion, but it's difficult to see how they can get an idea like *that* out of the Bible . . ."

Sound familiar? These are quotations from a well-known game called "evaluation." Other common pseudonyms for it are "Girl Talk," "Judging Others" and "Sanctified Slander." In it's most venomous form, it can turn into plain old gossip. It's a marvelous game—simple to learn and a perennial favorite. Any number can play and we usually all do to some extent. It's a game Christians play too well, as Paul points out.

ROMANS 14:1-12

[1]Accept Christians who are weak in faith, and don't argue with them about what they think is right or wrong. [2]For instance, one person believes it is all right to eat anything. But another believer who has a sensitive conscience will eat only vegetables. [3]Those who think it is all right to eat anything must not look down on those who won't. And those who won't eat certain foods must not condemn those who do, for God has accepted them. [4]Who are you to condemn God's servants? They are responsible to the Lord, so let him tell them whether they are right or wrong. The Lord's power will help them do as they should.

[5]In the same way, some think one day is more holy than another day, while others think every day is alike. Each person should have a personal conviction about this matter. [6]Those who have a special day for worshiping the Lord are trying to honor him. Those who eat all kinds of food do so to honor the Lord, since they give thanks to God before eating. And those who won't eat everything also want to please the Lord and give thanks to God. [7]For we are not our own masters when we live or when we die. [8]While we live, we live to please the Lord. And when we die, we go to be with the Lord. So in life

and in death, we belong to the Lord. [9]Christ died and rose again for this very purpose, so that he might be Lord of those who are alive and of those who have died.

[10]So why do you condemn another Christian? Why do you look down on another Christian? Remember, each of us will stand personally before the judgment seat of God. [11]For the Scriptures say, "As surely as I live," says the Lord, "every knee will bow to me and every tongue will confess allegiance to God."

[12]Yes, each of us will have to give a personal account to God.

TABOO OR NOT TABOO?

There's no doubt about it. The Christians in Rome were a diverse lot. They had a wide variety of backgrounds, from heathen paganism to Judaism. And they were surrounded by countless pagan customs and practices. They constantly faced questions on what a Christian should do about this or that.

Paul didn't try to "help" these early Christians out of their dilemma by sending them a detailed list of dos and don'ts. Instead, he gave them basic principles to guide Christian conduct and ethics.

For example, Paul deals in his letter with a problem that sounds strange today, but it certainly was very real for Roman Christians. It seems that some believers had their own set of pure food laws, and they strictly abstained from eating meat of any kind. These vegetarians looked askance at Christians who enjoyed steaks and roasts without a twinge of conscience. In other cases, it was the *kind* of meat that was called into question. For example, Jewish converts to Christianity were scandalized by the idea of eating pork. In addition, there was an even more sticky question: Was it right for a Christian to buy, serve or eat meat cut from animals used in pagan sacrifices? This "pagan meat" was sold every day at a good price after pagan rituals had been completed. It was good meat, too, as far as quality and taste were concerned. Only the best animals were used for sacrificial purposes.

Some Christians had no qualms about buying and eating the meat that was cut from animals offered to idols. To them idols were nothing more than carved pieces of wood or stone. The meat was unharmed, unchanged and perfectly good to eat. But other Christians were horrified by the idea. To them the meat that came from animals used in pagan rituals was "spiritually contaminated," certainly not fit for a true Christian's menu.

"To eat meat or not to eat meat" was no small question in the church at Rome. Some "anti-meat Christians" even doubted the salvation of their "less scrupulous" brothers in Christ. (Now the story is beginning to sound more familiar.)

There were other problems—such as on what day to worship (see Rom. 14:5-6). Some Christians thought they should use the already established religious holidays for worshiping God. Other sincere believers pointed out that all days were for worshiping God, so why designate certain days as more important?

So it went, and so it still goes. The disagreements are different, but the results are the same. We Christians don't see eye-to-eye, and so we judge one another. We evaluate, we criticize, we tear down—in a very spiritual way, of course. It is sort of a game, one version of which might be called "Helping Others to Be Spiritual":

"Have you heard about George spending all that money on his cabin in the mountains?"

"Why, yes, but he told me he was getting some good deals on materials."

"Maybe so, but think of how that money could be used to sponsor orphans or to send food to Third World countries."

Paul's advice on this kind of fun and games is brief: Don't do it. His logic is simple: You should not criticize another man's servant. All Christians are God's servants, so let the Holy Spirit convict them about where to spend their money (see Rom. 14:4).

Now, this is good advice, but a question remains. How do you apply this rule to specific situations? Are you supposed to be so agreeable that you become a regular "good-ole wishy-washy Charlie Brown"?

It helps if you understand what Paul is driving at in this passage. He is not saying that Christians can hold "poles apart" views on basic doctrines such as the deity of Christ or salvation by faith. Paul is talking about disputable questions, that is, questions where two points of view are equally valid and useful. To Paul the dispute over meat and holy days at Rome fell into this legitimately disputable category. And instead of ruling on who was right, Paul introduced a basic principle: There are many areas in life where the answer is not cut and dried or black and white. *Christians must search their own consciences to see what they really believe.* "Each person should have a personal conviction about [the] matter" (v. 5).

Another key point is the identity of the "weaker brother" Paul mentions in verse 1. Some Christians tend to call other believers "weak" if they violate their particular set of taboos. Is this what Paul meant by "weak"? In chapter 14, he makes it quite clear that his sympathies in the dispute on meat are with those who feel free to eat it, whether it was offered in a pagan sacrifice or not. Paul is saying that those who live in freedom and liberty to live above the legalistic taboos of men are not the weak ones. *The legalists are weak* and need to be accepted and understood.

There are two lessons here.

1. It is easy to blow up a marginal question until it is completely out of proportion (as many a church has learned to its misery). Majoring in minors is almost always the road to destruction.
2. It is easy to judge the other fellow and call him "weak" or "shallow" because he has a personal habit or idea that you don't agree with. But in reality *you* may be the weaker one because you are living legalistically (religiously) instead of in Christian freedom and liberty.

Paul may not lay down a list of dos and don'ts on disputable issues, but he is quite specific about the basic reason why Christians should stop nursing their pet taboos and start loving and accepting one another as brothers in Christ. *The Living Bible* puts it plainly: "We are not our own bosses to live or die as we ourselves might choose" (v. 7). The moment you begin criticizing someone else, you run the risk of slipping into the same sin that Adam committed: deciding you will become like God. Christians know that they are not the final authority for "living or dying we follow the Lord. Either way we are His" (v. 8, *TLB*).

Here is the key. It's our relationship with Christ that helps us understand why we shouldn't judge others. Who is first in the Christian's life? *Who is boss*? It is only as a Christian learns to let Christ be boss that he is able to live by His command to "love each other as I have loved you" (John 15:12, *NIV*).

And how do you show that you love the other fellow when you disagree with him? Actually, disagreements are key opportunities to practice Christian love. Christ was always willing to talk over a man's ideas with him. Here are some basic rules that the Lord taught and practiced. If you try to practice them, they will help you learn how to communicate with other people, instead of continuing to play judging games.

Be Genuine

In other words, be honest and open with other people. Be for real. Try dropping—a little at a time—your front, your spiritual mask, that vital piece of equipment for all Christian gamesmanship. The spiritual mask often has remarks like these coming from behind it:

"Yes, Lord willing, I hope to . . . "

"I just couldn't do that and take Jesus with me . . . "

"Before I do anything about this, I'll have to bathe the matter in prayer."

And, of course, all masks aren't spiritual. There is the "dripping with honey" (but it's really venom) mask; the "I've got confidence in *me*" mask; the "I've got *no* confidence in poor ole me" mask; and the well-known "reverse English" mask: "One thing about me—I'm *honest*."

How do you gain the nerve to start peeling away, layer by layer, the particular mask that you operate behind? The answer lies in your relationship to Christ—your real (unmasked) relationship. Bit by bit, as you build this relationship on sincere faith that openly seeks God's will, the mask or masks you need for "social security" become less essential. Instead of having a spirit of fear, you learn to be wise and strong, to love people and enjoy being with them (see 2 Tim. 1:7).

As you shed your mask, you become more genuine. You allow the Spirit of Christ to work in you, helping you to be sensitive and appropriate in your honesty and openness.

Appropriateness and sensitivity are vital to being genuine. Genuineness is not foolhardy frankness or asinine honesty. This is how judging, criticism and fighting often start. (After all, you only told the *truth*.) To paraphrase the old cliché, "Honesty that is guided and empowered by the Holy Spirit is the best policy." Or, as the Lord put it: "It is the man who shares my life and whose life I share who proves fruitful" (John 15:5, *Phillips*).

Be Accepting

People talk a lot about "accepting one another." What do they mean? Is it really as simple as saying, "I accept him, you understand, but I *can't stand* his attitude" (or his taste in clothes, his friends or his personal habits)?

All of us are self-conscious. Our image of self is directly related to how we feel, what we do, the things we like. Criticize a person's viewpoint, taste or ideas and you criticize *him*, no matter how much you may intend otherwise.

Before turning your guns (especially your spiritual guns) on someone's ideas, actions or attitudes, ask yourself a couple of questions: *Am I trying to help this person, or am I really trying to impose my value system? Do I respect and like this person for who he or she is, or am I trying to make him or her over to suit my idea of what is respectable, likable or spiritual?*

Does being accepting sound difficult? It is. But it helps the Christian to remember that God has accepted him—just as he is. And the One who said, "Come unto me" (Matt. 1:28) is also the One who said, "Stop judging superficially; you must judge fairly" (John 7:24, *Williams Translation*).[1]

Be Understanding

Acceptance doesn't mean much unless it is accompanied by understanding. What is understanding? Whatever it is, it is not "knowing something" about someone, having him all figured out or being able to predict what he will do. This kind of "understanding" says: "I understand what is *wrong* with you." This isn't real understanding; it is evaluation—the same Christian game that is the subject of this chapter.

REAL UNDERSTANDING IS EMPATHY—PUTTING YOURSELF IN THE OTHER PERSON'S SHOES...

Perhaps one fellow best described understanding when he stated on a questionnaire that if someone wanted to understand him, he should put himself "in my shoes"—I mean *really* put himself there.

This kind of understanding—putting yourself in the other person's shoes—is called empathy. When you show someone empathy, you mentally try to enter into the thoughts and ideas of the other person. That is, you try to see exactly how things seem to him or her.

You communicate empathy to other people more by your actions and facial expressions than you do by pat statements. For example, suppose someone disagrees with you on interpretation of a certain doctrine or verse in the Bible, or perhaps the disagreement is over something as simple as who will speak at the next get-together for your group. You can approach this disagreement in one of two basic ways. You can say by word, action or with as little as a slight curl of your lip: "You're all wet. Why don't you go hide and forget to come out?" Or you can try empathy and sincerely say: "You don't like that idea? Well, I think I see your point. Let's try to work out something else."

The above is not a magic formula. Some people are so biased, so fearful, so unaccepting, that they wouldn't know empathy if it shouted in their ear. But the point is that as you seek to acquire an attitude of understanding toward others, there is a better chance that you will experience less disagreement and do less judging, less criticizing. At least you have nothing to lose, except some of your pride, fear and defensiveness—and those other "cherished characteristics" that make us more religious than Christian.

Be genuine. Be accepting. Be understanding. These three simple rules were practiced and lived by the same Person who will one day judge us all. The best cure for criticism and judging others is to "remember, each of us will stand personally before the judgment seat of God . . . each of us will have to give a personal account to God" (Rom. 14:10,12).

FOR FURTHER THOUGHT

1. Memorize Romans 14:10. Next time you are tempted to criticize someone, spend a few moments in prayer, asking the Lord to produce in that person's life (and in yours) what is pleasing and acceptable to Him.

2. Reread Romans 14:1-12 and list several reasons why judging others is wrong.

3. Compare Romans 14:7-9 with 2 Corinthians 5:14-21; Galatians 2:20; Philippians 1:20-21. Write a statement that reflects what the lordship of Christ means to you.

4. Do you think the following statement is true or false? People often judge one another because of pride, fear or defensiveness. Write reasons for your answer.

CHAPTER 13

Stepping-Stone or Stumbling Block?

"Stepping-stone?" "Stumbling block?" What kind of religious jargon is this? Well, it isn't jargon really. The term "stumbling block" is a good solid biblical word, and it is also in Webster's, defined as "any cause of stumbling, perplexity, or error; any obstacle or impediment to steady progress." Paul has a few words on this idea of being an impediment to progress—specifically the progress of Christian growth in others. His solution is to become a "stepping-stone"—that is, to be willing to be walked on for the sake and love of Christ. Is Paul carrying this

Christian love idea past the Second Mile? See for yourself.

ROMANS 14:13—15:6

[13]So don't condemn each other anymore. Decide instead to live in such a way that you will not put an obstacle in another Christian's path.

[14]I know and am perfectly sure on the authority of the Lord Jesus that no food, in and of itself, is wrong to eat. But if someone believes it is wrong, then for that person it is wrong. [15]And if another Christian is distressed by what you eat, you are not acting in love if you eat it. Don't let your eating ruin someone for whom Christ died. [16]Then you will not be condemned for doing something you know is all right.

[17]For the Kingdom of God is not a matter of what we eat or drink, but of living a life of goodness and peace and joy in the Holy Spirit. [18]If you serve Christ with this attitude, you will please God. And other people will approve of you, too. [19]So then, let us aim for harmony in the church and try to build each other up.

[20]Don't tear apart the work of God over what you eat. Remember, there is nothing wrong with these things in themselves. But it is wrong to eat anything if it makes another person stumble. [21]Don't eat meat or drink wine or do anything else if it might cause another Christian to stumble. [22]You may have the faith to believe that there is nothing wrong with what you are doing, but keep it between yourself and God. Blessed are those who do not condemn themselves by doing something they know is all right. [23]But if people have doubts about whether they should eat something, they shouldn't eat it. They would be condemned for not acting

in faith before God. If you do anything you believe is not right, you are sinning.

¹We may know that these things make no difference, but we cannot just go ahead and do them to please ourselves. We must be considerate of the doubts and fears of those who think these things are wrong. ²We should please others. If we do what helps them, we will build them up in the Lord. ³For even Christ didn't please himself. As the Scriptures say, "Those who insult you are also insulting me." ⁴Such things were written in the Scriptures long ago to teach us. They give us hope and encouragement as we wait patiently for God's promises.

⁵May God, who gives this patience and encouragement, help you live in complete harmony with each other—each with the attitude of Christ Jesus toward the other. ⁶Then all of you can join together with one voice, giving praise and glory to God, the Father of our Lord Jesus Christ.

IT IS NOT WHAT YOU KNOW THAT COUNTS

In the first half of chapter 14, Paul teaches that we should not criticize or judge others, especially fellow Christians. In debatable matters each Christian is free to do whatever he or she feels is right, according to his or her own conscience. No Christian is to judge other Christians, because God will be the final judge of all (see Rom. 14:10,12).

But now, lest his readers become too intoxicated with the heady wine of liberty, Paul turns the coin over and introduces a sobering thought: *Freedom to follow convictions must be balanced by personal responsibility to do what is best for your brother in Christ.*

The question is not "Can I feel free to do this or that?" The question becomes "How can I fulfill my responsibility to help others live and grow in the Christian life?"

Christians are to live in such a way that they do not cause others to stumble, and this includes the pesky dispute concerning meat eaters versus vegetarians that Paul handled in Romans 14:1-12. Paul, who really sided with the meat eaters, turns around and says that even though people are free to eat meat if their consciences allow them to, they should not live in disregard for those whose consciences would be offended by a practice like eating meat (see v. 14). Paul did not want to misuse his freedom of conscience in any way that might tempt or influence believers around him to do something they felt was wrong, something that would damage their feelings of fellowship and rapport with Christ.

How do you apply this principle today? Christians do not disagree over eating meat, especially the kind of meat offered to idols. But Christians do disagree over a lot of things: from how to dress to hairstyles (and colors); from what is proper behavior on Sunday to what is proper entertainment; from what beverages a person may drink to what kind of job he or she may hold. And what is right in one part of the country is wrong in another. What is acceptable to one group is not acceptable to another, often in the same church. There is no universal outlook and no universal specific solution to these problems. There is, however, a universal principle to apply to them all: the principle that Paul has been discussing for the last several chapters—love.

In verse 15, Paul makes it clear: "If another Christian is distressed by what you eat, you are not acting in love if you eat it. Don't let your eating ruin someone for whom Christ died."

"Ruin someone for whom Christ died." When you look at it that way, the issue is no longer simply a disagreement between two sides or two points of view. Paul is actually saying that even

though your viewpoint may be perfectly valid, you still may have to "lose the battle" in order to win the war against evil as you fight for the good of others in the Body of Christ.

In these latter chapters of Romans, Paul emphasizes in various ways the challenge in Christian service: to glorify God, not yourself. In order to glorify God, Christians often must choose between satisfying their own preferences in favor of serving Christ. As Paul says, "Don't undo the work of God for a chunk of meat" (or for the sake of enjoying a certain pastime on Sunday afternoon, for the sake of looking "chic" in a certain style or for the sake of a favored form of entertainment). There may be nothing wrong with the meat (or its equivalent), but it is wrong to do anything that may cause a Christian brother or sister to stumble, to be confused, to be led away from Christ, instead of closer to Him.

Paul sums it up in verse 21: "Don't eat meat or drink wine or do anything else if it might cause another Christian to stumble."

Paul is saying that in many cases *what you know* is not the point; at the heart of the matter is *how you love* and how you help build others in the faith.

"All very good," you may say, "but is this kind of thing really so relevant for me today? Nobody I know harasses me about the things I do. I must be exempt from this stumbling-block business, or am I supposed to disconnect my cable because some Christians don't approve of HBO?"

Rest assured, Paul's words *are* relevant for today. For one thing, trying to regulate your life to please every Christian's idea of "taboo or not taboo" would be a great way to go insane. At best it would be the religiously laden path back to legalism, which is precisely what Paul is writing against in his letter to Rome. But what Paul is suggesting is that every Christian should be ready and willing to do what appears necessary to help another Christian within his or her sphere of influence.

Secondly, Paul is really not as concerned about "not being a stumbling block" as he is about "becoming a stepping-stone."

In so many words, then, Paul is saying that to not be a stumbling block is good but to seek to be a stepping-stone is even better. To be a stepping-stone means that you are actively in search of ways to help others draw closer to Christ. (Remember the "debt of love" in chapter 13? You never finish paying *that*.) Being a stepping-stone implies that you will be walked on. The idea of being walked on doesn't seem too appealing or glamorous—but then neither is getting crucified on the town garbage dump while cynics talk smut and soldiers curse and gamble for your clothes.

All right, let's say the principle is plain enough, but you're still left wondering: "*Just how* do I go about being a stepping-stone, not a stumbling block? How can I even find out who is stumbling over me? Do I go around church and take an opinion poll on my TV habits? Do I get up in prayer meeting and confess that I skipped Bible study to see *Gladiator*?"

Much more useful would be to first review the ideas on being genuine, accepting and understanding of others (see pp. 129-132). In addition, you might try working on being a *listener*—not at keyholes or on phone taps, but just in casual everyday conversations. In a word, *really listen* when people talk to you.

Listening has become a lost art. Lack of real listening is at the root of the poor communication that is prevalent today. Employees and employers don't really listen to one another. Teachers and students do not listen to each other and neither do parents and children. Everyone seems to have their transmitters on (to give their own opinions), but few seem willing to give their receivers a chance to really hear what others are trying to say.

For example, when did you last commit the error illustrated in the cartoon on page 141? Yesterday? This morning? Ten minutes ago? The situation is usually quite simple: Two people are talking. One is trying to explain his point of view, how he feels. Is the other person really listening to him? Not on your hearing aid! She is too busy thinking about what she's going to say in return. A lot of exchanges between people are not conversations; they are competitions, and may the loudest, most clever or most stubborn transmitter win.

Exactly what does listening have to do with being a stepping-stone? For one thing, perhaps people are sending you signals on your behavior, but you're not hearing them because you aren't trying. People do a lot of communicating indirectly, nonverbally. To get the full message from people, you often have to listen to *how* they are saying something, as well as the words themselves. Perhaps you have some friends who really *are* bothered by some of your habits or attitudes, but they would prefer to die before they would openly come out and admit it. They instead drop an occasional offhand remark, or perhaps they don't say anything, but their facial expression tells the story.

Many of us not only fail to listen to others, we also don't really see them either. Have you ever watched two people talking, and each is treating the other like a post? They look past one another, at the floor, at the ceiling, at the object they are working on or discussing but *seldom at each other*.

In order to be a good listener and looker, you need an attitude of empathy and understanding (see pp. 130-132). You *must want to hear* the other person before you can be willing to really listen. Listening is a practical, and much needed way of being a stepping-stone. Although some people aren't the easiest folk to listen to under any circumstances and many people are used to being talked at (or about), most of us are pleasantly surprised when someone is willing to talk *with us* and listen to what we are saying and feeling.

DO YOU REALLY LISTEN TO OTHERS, OR ARE YOU TOO BUSY THINKING OF WHAT YOU WILL SAY IN RETURN?

Try being a listener. Solomon was correct when he said: "What a shame, what folly, to give advice before listening to the facts!" (Prov. 18:13). The *New King James Version* says, "A wise man will hear and increase learning" (Prov. 1:5).

Real listening is also an excellent way to put 1 John 3:18 into action: "Let us stop just *saying* we love each other; let us *really show it* by our *actions*" (emphasis added). To love is to have the attitude of Christ toward others (see Rom. 15:5). This kind of attitude is willing to go out of its way, suffer inconvenience, *be stepped on* in order to serve and help. Christ's kind of love has no motive but the good of others; it expects nothing in return, because it only seeks to give.

But please note: Becoming a stepping-stone is not the same as being a doormat. To answer God's call for self-sacrificing service to others doesn't mean that you submit unquestioningly to abuse, ungodliness or persecution. There is a time for taking a stand, not out of pride or defensiveness, but to seek the good of all concerned, even when things get unpleasant.[1]

Christian service is not mechanical attention to duty. It is not a "legal obligation." Christian service—being a stepping-stone, not a stumbling block—has the highest possible motive: to glorify God. And when Christians truly serve with this purpose, they invariably reach out to those around them with concern and love—because God is love.

The Phillips's translation of Romans 15:5-7 sums it up this way:

> May the God who inspires men to endure, and gives them constant encouragement, give you a mind united with one another in your common loyalty to Christ Jesus. And then, as one man, you will sing from the heart the praises of God the Father of our Lord Jesus Christ. So open your hearts to one another as Christ has opened his heart to you, and God will be glorified.

FOR FURTHER THOUGHT

1. Memorize Romans 14:13. Then reread Romans 14:13-21 and write your own definition of "stumbling block" and "stepping-stone." Which is easier to be and why?
2. Try an experiment this week. Pick one or two people that you talk to but don't usually listen to very closely. Then as you interact with them during the week, really listen to what they say. Analyze how and why they say things, as well as their actual words. See if this improves your relationship with them. At the end of

the week, think about what you learned about being a stepping-stone instead of a stumbling block.

3. Compare Romans 15:1-6 with these verses on glorifying God: Psalm 22:23; Matthew 5:16; John 15:8; 1 Corinthians 6:18-20. What do you feel is your best means of glorifying God? Write down specific ideas and then spend a few moments in prayer, asking the Holy Spirit to help you live out these ideas in your daily routine and relationships.

CHAPTER 14

Divide or Multiply?

One of the marks of the early Christians was love. Celsus, anti-Christian Roman philosopher of the second century, had to grudgingly admit: "Behold, how these Christians love one another." And today . . . behold, how many Christians stay in their tight little cliques talking much of loving but not showing much unity in their living. Were the early Christians more spiritual than believers today? Did they possess some strange power that made them able to love one another constantly and consistently? Hardly. Loving one another didn't come any easier for the first Christians than it does for us. In fact, in some ways, it was harder. In the closing lines of his letter Paul includes some tips on how to be united around Christ. They are tips any Christian can use.

ROMANS 15:7-33

⁷So accept each other just as Christ has accepted you; then God will be glorified. ⁸Remember that Christ came as a servant to the Jews to show that God is true to the promises he made to their ancestors. ⁹And he came so the Gentiles might also give glory to God for his mercies to them. That is what the psalmist meant when he wrote: "I will praise you among the Gentiles; I will sing praises to your name."

¹⁰And in another place it is written, "Rejoice, O you Gentiles, along with his people, the Jews."

¹¹And yet again, "Praise the Lord, all you Gentiles; praise him, all you people of the earth."

¹²And the prophet Isaiah said, "The heir to David's throne will come, and he will rule over the Gentiles. They will place their hopes on him."

¹³So I pray that God, who gives you hope, will keep you happy and full of peace as you believe in him. May you overflow with hope through the power of the Holy Spirit.

¹⁴I am fully convinced, dear brothers and sisters, that you are full of goodness. You know these things so well that you are able to teach others all about them. ¹⁵Even so, I have been bold enough to emphasize some of these points, knowing that all you need is this reminder from me. For I am, by God's grace, ¹⁶a special messenger from Christ Jesus to you Gentiles. I bring you the Good News and offer you up as a fragrant sacrifice to God so that you might be pure and pleasing to him by the Holy Spirit. ¹⁷So it is right for me to be enthusiastic about all Christ Jesus has done through me in my service to God. ¹⁸I dare not boast of anything else. I have brought the

Gentiles to God by my message and by the way I lived before them. [19]I have won them over by the miracles done through me as signs from God—all by the power of God's Spirit. In this way, I have fully presented the Good News of Christ all the way from Jerusalem clear over into Illyricum.

[20]My ambition has always been to preach the Good News where the name of Christ has never been heard, rather than where a church has already been started by someone else. [21]I have been following the plan spoken of in the Scriptures, where it says, "Those who have never been told about him will see, and those who have never heard of him will understand."

[22]In fact, my visit to you has been delayed so long because I have been preaching in these places.

[23]But now I have finished my work in these regions, and after all these long years of waiting, I am eager to visit you. [24]I am planning to go to Spain, and when I do, I will stop off in Rome. And after I have enjoyed your fellowship for a little while, you can send me on my way again. [25]But before I come, I must go down to Jerusalem to take a gift to the Christians there. [26]For you see, the believers in Greece have eagerly taken up an offering for the Christians in Jerusalem, who are going through such hard times. [27]They were very glad to do this because they feel they owe a real debt to them. Since the Gentiles received the wonderful spiritual blessings of the Good News from the Jewish Christians, they feel the least they can do in return is help them financially. [28]As soon as I have delivered this money and completed this good deed of theirs, I will come to see you on my way to Spain. [29]And I am sure that when I come, Christ will give me a great blessing for you.

[30]Dear brothers and sisters, I urge you in the name of our Lord Jesus Christ to join me in my struggle by praying to God for me. Do this because of your love for me, given to you by the Holy Spirit. [31]Pray that I will be rescued from those in Judea who refuse to obey God. Pray also that the Christians there will be willing to accept the donation I am bringing them. [32]Then, by the will of God, I will be able to come to you with a happy heart, and we will be an encouragement to each other.

[33]And now may God, who gives us his peace, be with you all. Amen.

DO YOU DEAL IN POTENTIAL OR IN THE PAST?

At first glance these verses may appear to be sort of earthy, the tacked-on, final thoughts of a man who is hurrying to finish up what has been a rather long letter. There are, however, in what Paul writes some practical principles for Christian unity.

Have Hope

First, Paul had hope, even for the "hopeless" situations. In Romans 15:7-13, he touches once more on the "civil rights" problem of the Early Church: Jew versus Gentile. Jewish believers felt they had an inside track with God. After all, they were descendants of Abraham, members of a race that God chose to glorify His name and preserve His Word. Many Jews became Christian converts in the first years of the Church, and they held no little resentment and disdain for the "intrusion" of the Gentiles who also believed in Christ and wanted to be part of the Christian fellowship.

Some of the more zealous Jews tried to force Gentiles to go through "initiation ceremonies" like circumcision before they were allowed into the Church. It was hard for the good Jew, steeped in tradition, law and religion, to accept the idea that the gospel offered free salvation to all men on the basis of faith and faith alone. Many Jewish converts to Christianity did not completely accept or understand the concept of grace—God's unmerited love and favor. They preferred to keep Christianity in the religious category, garnished with requirements, rituals and rules.

The Gentiles, however, had little religious tradition and training. They came out of paganism, gladly accepting the idea that through Christ they could know forgiveness of sins and have salvation. They could not understand why the Jews made such a fuss, or why some Jewish believers seemed to look down on them because of their lack of religious training and background. There was a great deal of confusion, misunderstanding and friction because of this basic problem of Jew and Gentile in the same Christian congregation. This internal dispute was perhaps the greatest danger the Christian Church faced in its early years, and Paul knew it. That is why he deliberately designed his letter to the Romans (and another letter to the church in Galatia) to deal with the problem and explain why and how Christians should unite around the concept of salvation by faith in Christ.

Paul faced heavy odds and personal abuse of every kind in order to draw Christians together around Christ. Still, he kept going. A key to his perseverance is noted in Romans 15:13. If Paul could pray that the others would gain hope, peace and happiness from God, then he had experienced it himself. He experienced it *as he believed God*. He experienced hope and inner peace as he allowed the Holy Spirit's power to work in and through him—another example of the difference between being religious and being Christian.

Show Tact

And then, Paul had tact. You have to read between the lines a bit, but it is there. In Romans 15:14, he comments that he knows he really doesn't have to tell the Roman believers these basic things about love and glorifying God in a united fellowship. Paul doesn't nag them, bawl them out or drop sarcastic remarks. Paul prefers to "think positive" and look for the good in the situation. Paul was much more interested in *what a man could be than in what a man had been.*

Here is another key point. Think about it. Do you see other people in the process of becoming something better, or do you see them as bound by their past—what they have (or haven't) done or said (especially to you)? To put it plainly, do you carry a sanctified grudge against others in your family, your school or place of work? It is easy to stereotype others. You can place them

in neat little pigeonholes like "sloppy," "talkative," "dishonest," "undependable," "unfair," etc. But this is the way of religion, the way of the rules, the way of ideas and attitudes that are set in sanctimonious cement.

Christianity, however, deals in *potential*, in what a person can *become*, not only what he *is*. This is the heart of the gospel. If God had dealt with us strictly on the basis of our past, He would never have sent Christ to die for our sins. But God loved us. He saw us as persons of worth, of value, with potential. He forgave and He keeps on forgiving, always looking toward what we can become if we respond to the opportunity we have in Christ.

Meet Responsibilities

Paul showed love by meeting his responsibilities. Paul made his plans *around* his duties, not *on top* of them. He longed to go to Spain and carve still more frontier trails for the gospel (see Rom. 15:24). He hoped to make Rome a jumping-off place for his expansion of missionary activities to the west. But first, there was this rather routine but urgent matter of taking a gift of money to the Christians in Jerusalem (see v. 25). This gift was not some kind of bonus or special prize that the Jerusalem believers had won in a drawing. The money was badly needed for those who were down and out.

In a city like Jerusalem much of the available employment must have been connected with the Jewish Temple and the needs of this huge structure. But the Temple was controlled and run by the Sadducees, a sect of Jewish leaders who denied belief in the Resurrection and who were sworn enemies of Christ and Christianity. Many men in Jerusalem must have lost their jobs after becoming Christians.

Because of the Sadduceees and other zealous Jews who hated Christianity, Paul faced real danger in going to Jerusalem. As far as "old-time religion" Jews were concerned, Paul was public enemy number one. He was wanted everywhere, and above all in Jerusalem. The Jews had tried to kill Paul more than once (see Acts 14:5; 18:12), and now he was planning to go right into their main headquarters to deliver "care" packages!

Paul could have easily begged off. He could have sent someone else while he hurried on to "more important matters" at Rome or in Spain. But Paul not only preached Christian love and unity, he also practiced it. Paul's Lord had said, "Greater love has no one than this, than to lay down one's life for his friends" (John 15:13, *NKJV*). And because of his desire to help the poor in Jerusalem, Paul would eventually lay down his life.[1] Paul was a living, walking example of what it means to turn Christian words into Christian deeds.

Doesn't Christian unity, trust, mutual love and understanding really rest on this principle—deeds, not just words? If all Christians became persons of their word, what would happen?

Paul wasn't the only Christian who kept his word and labored hard and long for the unity of believers in the gospel. There were thousands like him, and a few of their names pop up at the very end of his letter to the Romans. There may not seem to be much practical help in this passage for facing the frustrations of the twenty-first-century technopolis. But there is an interesting thread of affirmation in chapter 16. See if you can trace it.

ROMANS 16:1-23

[1]Our sister Phoebe, a deacon in the church in Cenchrea, will be coming to see you soon. [2]Receive her in the Lord, as one who is worthy of high honor. Help her in every way you can, for she has helped many in their needs, including me. [3]Greet Priscilla and Aquila. They have been co-workers in my ministry for Christ Jesus. [4]In fact,

they risked their lives for me. I am not the only one who is thankful to them; so are all the Gentile churches. [5]Please give my greetings to the church that meets in their home.

Greet my dear friend Epenetus. He was the very first person to become a Christian in the province of Asia. [6]Give my greetings to Mary, who has worked so hard for your benefit. [7]Then there are Andronicus and Junia, my relatives, who were in prison with me. They are respected among the apostles and became Christians before I did. Please give them my greetings. [8]Say hello to Ampliatus, whom I love as one of the Lord's own children, [9]and Urbanus, our co-worker in Christ, and beloved Stachys.

[10]Give my greetings to Apelles, a good man whom Christ approves. And give my best regards to the members of the household of Aristobulus. [11]Greet Herodion, my relative. Greet the Christians in the household of Narcissus. [12]Say hello to Tryphena and Tryphosa, the Lord's workers, and to dear Persis, who has worked so hard for the Lord. [13]Greet Rufus, whom the Lord picked out to be his very own; and also his dear mother, who has been a mother to me.

[14]And please give my greetings to Asyncritus, Phlegon, Hermes, Patrobas, Hermas, and the brothers and sisters who are with them. [15]Give my greetings to Philologus, Julia, Nereus and his sister, and to Olympas and all the other believers who are with them. [16]Greet each other in Christian love. All the churches of Christ send you their greetings.

[17]And now I make one more appeal, my dear brothers and sisters. Watch out for people who cause divisions and upset people's faith by teaching things that are

contrary to what you have been taught. Stay away from them. [18]Such people are not serving Christ our Lord; they are serving their own personal interests. By smooth talk and glowing words they deceive innocent people. [19]But everyone knows that you are obedient to the Lord. This makes me very happy. I want you to see clearly what is right and to stay innocent of any wrong. [20]The God of peace will soon crush Satan under your feet. May the grace of our Lord Jesus Christ be with you.

[21]Timothy, my fellow worker, and Lucius, Jason, and Sosipater, my relatives, send you their good wishes.

[22]I, Tertius, the one who is writing this letter for Paul, send my greetings, too, as a Christian brother.

[23]Gaius says hello to you. I am his guest, and the church meets here in his home. Erastus, the city treasurer, sends you his greetings, and so does Quartus, a Christian brother.

HOW WILL YOUR ONE-SENTENCE SUMMARY READ?

This chapter almost makes you feel like you've broken into someone's desk and rifled some of her personal papers. Paul is talking directly to friends now, and behind many of his brief comments are dramas that were never written, as well as heroics and sacrifices that were never recorded. Bible scholars have done a great deal of speculating on just who these people were, where they came from and what eventually happened to them. A most useful observation, however, is the one by William Barclay, who comments that in these verses Paul characterizes many of these people in a single sentence.[2] "They risked their lives for me" (Rom. 16:4). "He was a good man" (v. 10). "He was a hard worker" (v. 12). If your friends or family were asked to sum you up in one sentence, what would that sentence be?

For Further Thought

1. Review the three principles for promoting Christian unity talked about in this chapter: Have hope, show tact and meet responsibilities. Can you think of specific ways that you can apply these principles to your life? List at least one idea for each principle.

2. Think of someone you have labeled as "undependable," "sloppy," "no personality," "moody," "grumpy," etc. Then write down some ideas on what you can do to treat this person in a more positive way. What can you do to see them as not bound by their past but with potential to change and grow in the future? Commit to praying daily for that person this week, asking the Holy Spirit to bear His fruit in that person's life.

3. Memorize Romans 15:13. Do a short word study on what the Bible says about hope by summarizing the following verses in your own words: Proverbs 14:32; John 3:3; Colossians 1:5; Titus 2:13; 1 Peter 1:3. On what do Christians base their hope? Is hope essential to a Christian's daily life? Why?

4. What one-sentence summary could be written about you today? Write it down and spend a few moments in prayer, asking God to help you live up to your full potential as His child.

Never Look Back

Paul's handbook on how to be a Christian without being religious is about to close.

You may or may not agree with the *definitions* of "Christian" and "religious." But the book of Romans emphasizes that there is a definite *difference*.

According to Webster's, a religion is a system of faith and of worship.

And a Christian does have that.

According to Webster's, a religion is the service and adoration of God expressed in forms of worship.

And a Christian certainly does this.

According to Webster's, religion is devotion, fidelity, conscientiousness, an awareness or conviction of the existence of a supreme being, which arouses reverence, love, gratitude, the will to obey and serve.

A Christian has all this too, and one thing more.

The Christian has power.

And it's not a power he generates from within himself. He knows that what the Bible claims is true: A man's heart is deceitful, a check that keeps bouncing no matter how neatly he writes on it.

A Christian's power comes from God—Someone beyond himself. Religion creates a "someone" or a "something" tailored to size, not too big of course. Religion produces a God that is easy enough to handle and compact enough to tuck away in the dresser drawer between Sundays. But Christianity doesn't talk about this kind of God.

Christianity talks about a God that you can't keep at arm's length by "reaching out for Him." Christianity claims that God reached out to us and did something for all mankind: *He removed our guilt.* Outside of death, guilt is perhaps man's greatest enemy. Guilt is the gnawing, corrosive acid that eats at a person from inside, the instinctive knowledge that you aren't all you would have the rest of the world believe you are, that you really aren't fit to stand before a righteous, holy God.

Search the tomes of the religions, the cults, the sects. None of them truly claims to have an answer for sin and guilt. Many groups explain guilt away quite neatly by refusing to admit it is there. You'll have to make up your own mind about that. You'll have to consider the evidence: the pages of history, especially recent history, that record wars, genocide, mass destruction and the surreal insanity of airliners flying into the World Trade Center, killing thousands. Or turn to the pages of your local newspaper where murder, rape, robbery and countless other crimes are reported daily. If you're still not convinced, be honest and consult your own experience, your own score in the game of life.

It all leaves us with one real claim to fame. We are all capable of self-delusion and deceit, of chicanery and cruelty far beyond the imagination.

Someone commits murder or suicide. Someone gets mixed up in dope, winds up having an abortion or just plain double-crosses a good friend. We are shocked. We never thought a person as fine as "so-and-so" would be capable of *that*. But we are all capable. We are all sinners who have fallen short of the glory of God.

Christianity deals honestly with this basic problem of sin and guilt. Christianity says the living God entered history. The Bible's clear teaching is that God became human flesh. He died on the cross, not as a misunderstood itinerant preacher who didn't get the breaks, but as a Supreme Sacrifice to pay the penalty for all sin. And that wasn't all. The Bible plainly states that Christ rose from the dead. His followers saw not a ghost, not a figment of their imagination, but a risen body that could be touched, that even ate food.

Either all this is truth (not "myth"), or Christianity is the supreme hoax of history, not even fit to be called a "great religion." But if Christianity is not more than a mere religion, then it is not worth the paper that the New Testament is printed on.

And perhaps the strangest thing of all is that God has given all of us the freedom to treat Him as we please. God entered history, yes, but He hardly took us by force. A stable is not the usual setting for a coronation. A cross is not the usual spot for a farewell address.

And so, if you wish, you can keep Christianity in the religion category. You can refuse to believe any of its amazing claims. You can classify it with the quaint folklore of Greek mythology. You can relegate it to the escapism of the Buddhists and Hindus. You can be generous and say it is filled with the wisdom of Taoism or Confucius.

It doesn't matter how you want to disbelieve. The results are the same. You remain captain of your fate. You keep God cut down to a comfortable size, something you can handle, something that doesn't become inconvenient. Actually, you worship a replica of your own god—yourself. In effect, you tell the true God, "I don't need any help." And you don't get any.

But there's the other way to reduce Christianity to a religion—from the inside. Instead of refusing the gospel, you accept it. You "get saved." You join the Church. You worship every Sunday with the fellowship of the redeemed.

But despite your claim to faith in God's grace, you mix being a Christian with being religious. You couch it in warm spiritual tones, but you feel your relationship to God still depends on how well you follow the rules and regulations. In short, it's still a matter of how well you perform, how high you reach.

Many a Christian looks at Christian living like a pole vaulter eyes the "20-foot barrier."[1] He works on his form. That is, he gets his praying down pat; he learns the right clichés and how to quote the favorite proof texts at the right psychological moment. He constantly tries to find the springiest pole he can. That is, he is always looking for the new spiritual giant with whom he can identify and thereby somehow have some of his spirituality rub off on him. And naturally, like any good vaulter, he practices diligently, showing up at all the meetings and services and making sure he looks and sounds as spiritual as the next guy. But inside he doesn't really feel that he can ever do 20 feet. He still equates Christianity with "being good," and he just doesn't feel he'll ever be good enough.

Well, in one sense this kind of Christian is right: He isn't "good enough," and he never will be as long as he goes at it that way. To go back to the pole-vault comparison for a second, the bar is not just 20 feet up. It's 1,000 feet high and all the poles are toothpicks. Being a Christian is not a matter of making all the right moves or earning biblical brownie points and spiritual merit badges.

Being a Christian is a matter of personal faith and commitment to Jesus Christ.

Yes, you've *heard* that before. But have you really *thought* about it? Remember how Peter tried walking on the water (see Matt. 14:22-32)? He did fine until he took his eyes off Christ, until he looked back and started getting nervous over the size of the waves. He started to sink, and he wound up crying, "Lord, save me!" (Matt. 14:30). This is a perfect illustration of the daily choices we make that result in our being Christian or being religious. You can live by faith, in a personal commitment to Christ, or you can look back, forget about Him . . . and sink.

Like most of life, it's not completely "either-or." Most of us never completely sink, but we don't ride the top of the waves all the time either. A lot of the time we seem to sort of wade through life—up to our knees, waist or neck in circumstances, self-will and frustration.

In other words, we Christians seem to be incurably religious, constantly tempted to tack on the religious flourish, live by the rules or add just a bit of self-effort that puts our personal touch on things.

But God doesn't need our personal touch. He wants *us* and leaves the striving to Him.

One thing that helps is to remember that Christianity is not a state of perfection. In Romans, Paul tells you how to have victory over sin, but he doesn't tell you how to be perfect. Paul knew that being a Christian is not a destination. A Christian has not "arrived." Christianity is a *walk*, a way of life, a process of maturity.

Go back and read the high point of Paul's letter to Rome: chapter 8. The Christian cannot be separated from the love of Christ. The Christian *can* have victory. The Christian life *does* work, *as you follow after the Holy Spirit.*

If you want a summary of what it means to be a Christian without being religious, memorize Romans 8:5: "Those who are dominated by the sinful nature think about sinful things, but those who are controlled by the Holy Spirit think about things that please the Spirit."

And as you please the Spirit, *you please yourself.*

It isn't always easy. It isn't automatic. The Christian life means growth and change. Growth and change are often painful, and not everyone grows at the same rate. But as Christians grow, they shed their religious facades and kindergarten concepts of God. They take on the attitude of hope and confidence that Paul shows in his closing lines of Romans.

Christians are committed to an almighty God in faith and obedience. Christians are in touch with Christ through the Holy Spirit who dwells in them. Christians are on speaking terms with their Lord. They do not pray once a month, once a week or even once a day to a God that is a relative stranger.

You can always tell when two people really know each other—when they really communicate. There is a relaxed, comfortable atmosphere. There is no stiffness, no stuffiness, yet there is respect, trust, love.

If you're a Christian who hopes to scrape off the religious scales, you seek this kind of relationship as you rely on the power of the life-giving Spirit, the power that is yours through Christ Jesus, the power that has freed you from the vicious circle of sin and death (see Rom. 8:2, *TLB*). As you live your Christian life, you may slip. You may fail. You may sometimes sink a bit, but your goal is always to not merely follow a religion. You have a hope, a power and a potential that come from beyond yourself. You are growing, changing, becoming all that God has in mind for you to be. You continually learn to trust, listen to and glorify the Living God.

And you never look back . . .

ROMANS 16:25-27

[25]God is able to make you strong, just as the Good News says. It is the message about Jesus Christ and his plan for you Gentiles, a plan kept secret from the beginning of time. [26]But now as the prophets foretold and as the eternal God has commanded, this message is made known to all Gentiles everywhere, so that they might believe and obey Christ. [27]To God, who alone is wise, be the glory forever through Jesus Christ. Amen.

Endnotes

Chapter 1

1. Dr. David Block, "For Heaven's Sake: A Jewish Astronomer's Odyssey," *Issues 7:8,* 2001. http://www.jfjonline.org/pub/issues/07-08/heavenssake.htm (accessed November 27, 2001).
2. For biographical information about Dr. Ross, visit his website at http://www.reasons.org/about/staff/ross/html.
3. Hugh Ross, "Astronomical Evidences for the God of the Bible," *Reasons to Believe,* 2001. http://reasons.org/resources/papers/astroevid.html (accessed November 27, 2001).
4. B. K. Kuiper, *The Church in History* (Grand Rapids, MI: Wm. B. Eerdmans Publishing Co., 1964), p. 162.
5. Justo Gonzalez, *The Story of Christianity* (Peabody, MA: Prince Press, 1984), vol. 2, pp. 16-17.
6. Ibid., p. 19.
7. For an excellent biography of Martin Luther, read Roland Bainton, *Here I Stand* (Nashville, TN: Abingdon, 1954).

Chapter 2

1. Compare Romans 2:24 and Isaiah 52:5 in the *King James Version* of the Bible. Note that both verses speak of God's name being blasphemed because of religious hypocrisy.

Chapter 3

1. Ann Hogedorn Auerbach, *Ransom: The Untold Story of International Kidnapping* (New York: Henry Holt and Company, 1998), p. 481.
2. Auerbach, "We Have Your CEO. Hand Over $50 Million," *BusinessWeek,* August 10, 1998. http://www.businessweek.com/1998/32/b3590042.htm (accessed November 27, 2001).
3. Read Romans 4:1-5 and Genesis 15:6 in the *King James Version* of the Bible. Note that Romans 4:3 is a quote from Genesis 15:6, explaining that Abraham's faith was "counted unto him for righteousness."
4. Commander Neil Armstrong's historic words were broadcast live on July 20, 1969. The Apollo 11 mission was the first successful attempt to reach the moon.

Chapter 4

1. "Quarterback Kurt Warner Plans to Use Fame for Evangelism," *Maranatha Christian Journal*, November 29, 2001. http://www.mcjonline.com/news/00/20000204a.htm (accessed November 29, 2001).
2. Dr. Richard C. Halverson, *Perspective* (September 1966), n.p.
3. Wayne Gruden, *Systematic Theology* (Grand Rapids, MI: Zondervan Publishing House, 1994), pp. 494-496. See also John Stott, *Romans: God's Good News for the World* (Downers Grove, IL: InterVarsity Press, 1994), pp. 149-154. As Stott points out, some theologians have emphasized that all of us who follow Adam are copying his example; other scholars stress our depraved nature, which we inherited from Adam. While recognizing the partial truths in these views, Stott believes the primary meaning of Romans 5:12-21 is that we all sinned in and through Adam, because he was the representative or "federal head" of the entire human race.

Chapter 5

1. Lawrence O. Richards, *Expository Dictionary of Bible Words* (Grand Rapids: Zondervan Publishing House, 1985), p. 543.
2. Ibid., p. 542. See also Everett F. Harrison, ed., *Baker's Dictionary of Theology* (Grand Rapids: Baker Book House, 1960), pp. 470-471.

Chapter 6

1. Nicole Johnson, "Reigns Without Crown," *Christianity.com*, 2001. http://www.christianity.com/CC/article/0,,PTID1000|CHID74|CIID142201,00.html (accessed December 21, 2001).

Chapter 7

1. Ralph Carmichael, "We Are More Than Conquerors" (Waco, TX: Bud John Songs, Inc., 1985).

Chapter 9

1. Francis Thompson, *The Hound of Heaven* (Harrisburg, PA: Morehouse Publishing, 1986), n.p.
2. Alan Redpath, *Getting to Know the Will of God* (Downers Grove, IL: InterVarsity Press, 1954), p. 1.
3. Ibid., p. 12.

Chapter 11

1. An excellent resource for information about the Church during this time is William Barclay, *The Letter to the Romans* (Louisville, KY: Westminster John Knox Press, 1975).

Chapter 12

1. Charles B. Williams, trans., *The New Testament: A Private Translation in the Language of the People* (Chicago: Moody Press, 1957), p. 217.

Chapter 13

1. Paul himself did this on numerous occasions. See Acts 16:16-40; 22:23-29; 26:19-32. See also both of Paul's letters to the Corinthians.

Chapter 14

1. Paul never left Jerusalem a free man. The Jews tried to kill him; he was saved by Roman arrest, eventually transported to Rome under guard and was finally executed by order of Caesar.
2. For more information about these individuals, see William Barclay, *The Letter to the Romans* (Louisville, KY: Westminster John Knox Press, 1975).

Conclusion

1. As of February 2002, the only man to have cleared 20 feet was Sergey Bubka, who did it on at least 10 occasions. Bubka, from the Ukraine, set the world indoor-pole-vault record at 20'1" in 1993. He also holds the outdoor record of 20'1¾", which he set in 1994. Information from Tim Footman, ed., *Guiness World Records 2001* (New York: Bantam Books, 2001), p. 354.

Truly Life-Transforming Reading

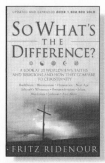
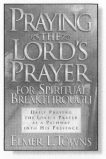
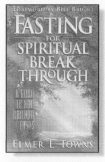

Let the Spirit Lead Your Life

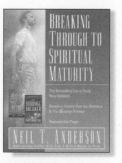

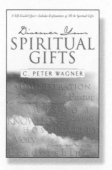

OSF
683 5000
691 - 1000 Proc
672 5522 neth